THE Unreformed MARTIN LUTHER

A Serious (and Not So Serious) Look at the Man Behind the Myths

ANDREAS MALESSA

Kregel
Publications

ISBN 978-0-8254-4456-2

Printed in the United States of America
17 18 19 20 21 22 23 24 25 26 / 5 4 3 2 1

Contents

Foreword

The greats of history seem to have one thing in common: however dramatic their lives, inevitably legends, myths, and fables are added to the historical record, either by tradition or the intent of biographers. Gnostic authors added ridiculous details to the life of Jesus of Nazareth, much as Parson Weems did centuries later, with more noble intentions, to George Washington.

Martin Luther was no exception. Both friends and foes added unhistorical addenda to the facts of his life. This book by German author Andreas Malessa is a collection of many of the most familiar stories about Luther. Perhaps the most controversial is his claim that when Luther stood before Emperor Charles V, he did not crown his defiant defense with the famous words, "Here I stand. I cannot do otherwise"—since court reporters did not preserve these words and they are only attested much later. (John Foxe, a younger contemporary of Luther, wrote in his famous *Book of Martyrs* that Luther closed his defense with the words, "Here I stand and rest. May God have mercy on me"—which may lend authenticity to this traditional statement after all.)

Debunkers can certainly be killjoys. But they are necessary to keep truth about the past clear and accurate. These pages are no hostile assault on the life of Luther. On the contrary, they often correct the record on the cruder myths generated by his opponents, such as the claim that Luther was a drunkard, a liar, and even someone who ate at the pulpit while preaching.

Anything but a rehash of Luther's life, this book is immensely readable and well crafted, and will provoke laughter on nearly every page—thanks to Luther's own blazing sense of humor and to the Hillman son-father team's skillful translation and adaptation of the original German edition.

Martin Luther's colorful life story has no need for embellishments of any kind since facts alone qualify his as one of the most dramatic in history. He was "The Man of the Second Millennium," a towering figure who changed the world. This embattled ex-monk had to fight on two fronts for the rest of his life: against the medieval Catholic Church on the right, which excommunicated him for daring to reform the church, and the radical revolutionaries on the left, who claimed that Luther had not gone far enough. All the while he accomplished what seemed impossible: tearing down unbiblical traditions but rebuilding the church, thus doing the work of half a dozen theologians. Such a life needs no enhancements whatever. Bravo to Andreas Malessa for identifying the enduring greatness of Luther.

PAUL L. MAIER
Professor (Emeritus) of History
Western Michigan Univerisity

Preface

When someone becomes a famous personality, adored by millions of fans and puffed up by the media, they inescapably achieve star status (or at least become a celebrity of sorts). And predictably, as celebration gives way to cynicism, the entertainment press and investigative journalists want to peel back the public mask and reveal the "real" person. Reporters try to find (or invent) weaknesses, mistakes, and, preferably, scandals. The rule seems to be: "First the hype, then the story." So run the daily ups and downs in the entertainment excitement curve.

Historians are already in one sense investigative journalists when it comes to Martin Luther, but the public face of Luther—the mythic Luther—has been shaped by many others. In serious, academic tones (like historians)—but using methods similar to that of journalists—the media, the church, and the culture-shapers have created this great historical figure, a Luther gilded in polished gold. That will certainly be the case during this year, the five-hundredth anniversary of the Reformation. The Luther hype will predictably lead a handful of professional historians to say, "Well, it was actually totally different."

I'm not an investigative journalist—and neither do I want to be—and although I like church history and theology, that's not where I began my research on Luther. I have asked students and teachers, workers and retirees, friends and colleagues, what they know about Martin Luther and the Reformation. I have come across legends, horror stories, terribly wrong quotes, and, above all, many little half-truths and funny myths. I have noted all of them. And with them and my responses to them, I would like to inform (as well as amuse) you. Yes, and perhaps also shock you—the sixteenth century is not for the faint of heart.

The Weimar edition of Martin Luther's complete works includes all his books, Bible commentaries, sermons, table talks, lectures, essays, leaflets, and records. The Weimar edition is about eighty thousand pages long, bound in 121 volumes. There are 2,585 letters that Luther wrote and 926 letters that were written to him. There are so many texts that one could prove almost anything about Luther as well as furnish the respective counterargument with quotes from his contemporary friends and enemies. It's not hard to find evidence to corroborate the view that Luther was all of these:

the traumatized child and the respectful son
the self-tormenting ascetic and the tippler
the vulgar churl and the sophisticated poet
the affectionate husband and the domineering macho man
the popular speaker and the intellectual genius

The complexity of Luther's personality only increases when other characterizations are considered:

Luther the sly politician
Luther the pious prayer
Luther the free thinker

Luther himself already knew what would happen after his death: "Now everyone wants to be heard first and each wants to spill out their thoughts. On this topic the preacher Solomon said rightly, 'of making many books there is no end!' You will still be amazed, when I lie in the ground, how many books will be written about me."[1]

---

1. Krumbholz, *Euch stoßen*, 28.

I acknowledge my own guilt in this accusation. So, have I distilled here the "real" Luther by pulling back the mask and discovering the man beyond the myths? Most likely not—at least not completely. But perhaps by the end of this short investigation, you will be curious about which thoughts and feelings, which life experiences and God experiences, of this very distant man are very near to us today, and still affect and concern us in the five-hundredth anniversary of Luther's historic actions in Wittenberg. If so, I will be very happy indeed.

ANDREAS MALESSA

Portrait of Martin Luther, 1525, by Lucas Cranach the Elder (1472–1553)
National Museum of Fine Art, Stockholm, Sweden

THE Unreformed MARTIN LUTHER

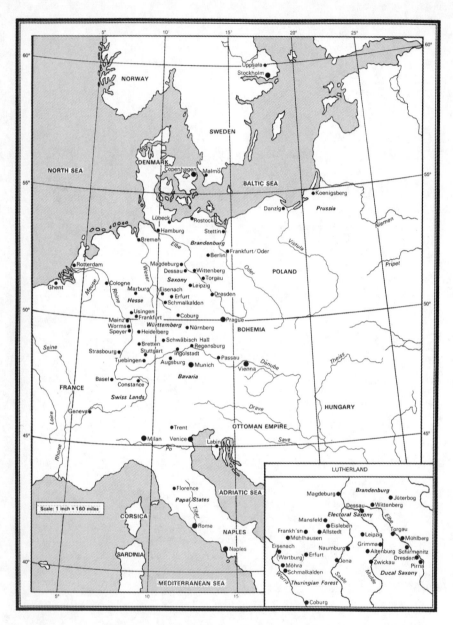

Central Europe in the time of the Reformation

Chapter 1

Luther Was a Superstitious Person

W as Martin Luther superstitious? If so, he would be in good company. In March 2014 the Evangelical Church in Germany published their fifth sociological church member study titled *Commitment and Indifference*. The survey results showed that 14.8 percent of evangelicals believe in amulets, stones, or crystals, and 22 percent have an affinity for astrology. Of those who attend church weekly, 22 percent believe in the power of stones or jewels, while only 12 percent of those who never or rarely (less than once a year) attend services hold a similar view.[1] So according to this study, "worldly" forms of religions are more likely inside the church than outside the church. Churchgoers are more superstitious than nonchurchgoers.

Not to be outdone, more than 25 percent of Americans admit to being very or somewhat superstitious when it comes to knocking on wood, walking under a ladder, breaking a mirror, or having a black cat cross one's path.[2] And when categorized by religious affiliation, 20 to 30 percent of Catholics and Protestants believe in these common superstitions.[3] On the other hand, atheists and agonistics come in significantly lower

---

1. "Engagement und Indifferenz," Evangelische Kirche in Deutschland.
2. Moore, "One in Four Americans Superstitious."
3. "Superstitions Held by Americans in 2014," Statista.

at 18 percent and below—which must be convenient for them when it comes to cats and ladders.

Here one is tempted to quote Luther, somewhat tongue-in-cheek, although Luther meant it seriously: "I do not want to prophesy about the future of Germany based on the stars, but I dismiss it to the wrath of God from theology! It is impossible that Germany will get off without a hard punishment."[4] That certainly sounds like Luther had no truck with astrology and assorted superstitions.

So was Martin Luther, the stalwart leader of the Reformation, superstitious or not? As best as can be known, the answer is yes, he was. This is not a fallacy about Luther, but a fact—and he sometimes had a bad conscience about it, ironically.

The worldview of the medieval mind was magical, mystical, and full of menacing puzzles. Nature was populated with angels, devils, witches, fairies, trolls, and undead, as well as half-human, half-animal creatures. Culture was full of oracles, secrets, fates, and taboos. Houses and clothes were decorated with and protected by powerful amulets and symbols. Esoteric mutterings, alleged secret lore, the spirituality of natural powers—all were self-evident and common sense in the spiritual climate of the time.

Martin's mother, Margarete Luther (born Lindemann), was from a small village. Her daughter died suddenly of cot death (now called SIDS). Margarete was firmly convinced that a neighbor was an evil witch who had cursed her little Magdalene. When the suspected woman was beaten to death and laid on the village green, Martin's mother expressed no dismay, but rather relief. According to her, "Satan took back one of his own."[5]

Later in Luther's life—some twenty-three years after Wittenberg had become the center of the Reformation—a woman named Prista Frühbottin was burned to death in the Wittenberg market square on June 29, 1540. The accusation: weather magic and pasture poisoning (two sorts of crimes the modern mind certainly must puzzle over!). Lucas Cranach the Younger, a German Renaissance artist, even painted the scene of her

---

4. Schilling, *Luther zum Vergnügen*, 170.
5. Süßenguth, *Aus einem traurigen Arsch*, 16.

execution as a kind of old-school crime photojournalist, so to speak. So it's safe to say that Luther and Wittenberg were hardly sociopolitically enlightened in our modern sense of the term.

The Catholic theologian and Frankfurt capitular (Catholic administrator) Johann Cochläus claimed in his 1549 biography of Luther that the good-looking Margarete Lindemann amused herself passionately with the devil and thereby conceived the baby Martin (no doubt his opponents thought Luther was a cheeky devil already). Not surprisingly for the times, this slander was not discounted even among the educated class as tasteless nonsense but was discussed as a serious possibility.

Luther himself believed in similar ideas: "Prussia is full of devils, and in Lappland there are many wizards. In Switzerland there is a sea on a high mountain, which they call Pilatus Sea—there is where the devil rampages. Near my home, there is a pond on top of Pichel Mountain. When one throws a stone in the pond, a large storm emerges."[6] Luther not only personally believed these ideas but he stated them publicly.

From May 1521 until March 1522 Luther had to hide himself in the Wartburg, a castle in the town of Eisenach. Luther was on his way home after his legendary defense of his writings at the Diet of Worms.[7] Martin Luther's friends "kidnapped" him so the trip back home would not end with Luther being burned at the stake. He lived in a part of the spacious fortress that was only reachable by a set of folding attic stairs. Twice a day he was provided with something to eat by two servants who only knew that he was a foreigner with the name Sir George.

Luther was lonely—but evidently not alone. He thought that there was a poltergeist in his room:

> Now they had brought me a sack of hazelnuts, which I ate and locked in a chest. When I went to bed at night, the poltergeist

---

6. Krumbholz, *Euch stoßen*, 42.
7. While this phrase can hardly be read in English without a bit of a smirk, a "diet" was a deliberative assembly, in this case of the Holy Roman Empire with Emperor Charles V presiding. It was held in the city of Worms, which was an imperial city.

came to me for the hazelnuts—with one hand after the other he pounded on the wood very hard, troubling me in the bed. And when I finally got a little sleep, the thing made such a rumble on the stairs, it was as if someone had thrown a dozen barrels down the stairs. I knew, of course, that the stairs were locked and protected with chains and iron so that no one could throw barrels up and down the stairs. I woke up and wanted to see what was there, but the stairs were locked. Then I said, 'If you're there, so be it then!' I commend me to the Lord Christ, of whom it is written, 'omnia subiecisti pedibus eius' ['you have everything under your feet'], as it reads in Psalm 8, verse 6. And then I went back to bed.[8]

Luther's courageous stand against the poltergeist alone at night in a castle attic may well amaze us today. For some, it brings out a sense of pious wonder—"There you can just see how secure he was in Jesus, just how steadfast this man of faith was!"

Then again, one can also interpret this from a religious and psychological point of view and say, "There you can see how naturally and self-confidently he dealt with manifestations of the supernatural."

Another person could just as well explain this with a dry sobriety and say, "A sack full of hazelnuts can attract mice or may have already contained some. They were rustling around and obviously creating a startling commotion."

Or one can be amazed that anyone would take this story at face value at all. They might say, "Of course, Luther told this story years later during his famous 'table talks,'[9] and perhaps, to add a little more interest, he exaggerated in the retelling a little bit." If so, he would not be the first preacher of the gospel who believed a little exaggeration never hurt a good story!

---

8. Krumbholz, *Euch stoßen*, 38.
9. Not talks about tables, but short sermons delivered around meal times. More on them in chapter 7.

If Luther had ever been challenged about this story, he could have mentioned another person who was awakened by the poltergeist in the same room in the castle: the wife of the captain of the castle, Madame von Berlepsch, who occasionally lived separated from her husband in 1521. Luther says, "Then came Hans von Berlepsch's wife toward Eisenach and sensed that I was in the castle, and would have really liked to have seen me. However, it couldn't be. They brought me into another chamber and put up the same woman from Berlepsch in my chamber. There, she heard such a rumble in the night that she thought there were a thousand devils inside."[10]

However, with this "chief witness" of the Wartburg poltergeist, Luther's account becomes somewhat suspicious. How likely is it that one would accommodate a noble lady, of all people, in a secluded and haunted room? Why did she not stay the night in the luxurious chamber of her husband? That points to a seemingly ended marriage. How did Luther know about the lady of Berlepsch's experience when it officially "couldn't be" that they could encounter one another? From what we know, those questions have no satisfactory answer.

However, there may be another explanation for all this turmoil in the tower. We know from Luther's letters during this period that he suffered terribly from loneliness and from sexual desires, a troubling experience, no doubt, for a celibate monk. "I'm burning in the great fire of my untamed flesh. I should be rutting in spirit as I am in the flesh."[11] As Luther struggled against the seductive torments of sexual thoughts, did his own inner psychological struggles intensify his perception of the havoc among the hazelnuts? Perhaps, but we don't know.

As early as the late 1520s, however, a distinction between a more critical and rationally minded Luther and the medieval, magically minded, and superstitious Luther was becoming apparent, typically with the Bible as the instrument of this demystification. "The devil cannot frighten me so much that I break out in sweat during sleep. I don't worry about the

---

10. Krumbholz, *Euch stoßen*, 38; Wolf, *Luther*, 222.
11. Diwald, *Luther*, 246.

dreams or omens. I have the Word of God. That is enough for me. I also don't want an angel to come to me. I would not believe him now."[12]

Also with respect to faith in horoscopes and the anxious following of constellations, Luther developed a critical distance, but not due to scientific reasons: "Signs and stars were not therefore created to master me, but for my benefit and service. Night and day they shall rule, but over my soul they shall have neither rule nor power. The sky was made to give light and time. The earth to support and feed us."[13] Casually expressed: stars are created, not creating. So with age, Luther gained a somewhat critical distance from superstition. He would later write, "There is nothing more powerful in the world as superstition, but before God it's an abomination."[14]

> "The devil cannot frighten me so much that I break out in sweat during sleep. I don't worry about the dreams or omens. I have the Word of God."

Interestingly, a close friend of Luther's—a very intelligent, accomplished linguist, and almost always a very rational person—cared a lot about astrology: Philip Melanchthon.[15] "He interprets a lot from astrology," Luther observed. Melanchthon was so influenced by the recommendations and warnings of his personal horoscope that he refused to cross the wooden bridge over the Elbe River in the city of Wittenberg with Luther one day because his horoscope forbade it. The more practical Luther suggested they stop by a pub on the near side of the Elbe instead. Luther, quite unsuperstitiously, later said, "Philip Melanchthon

12. Schilling, *Luther zum Vergnügen*, 40.
13. Krumbholz, *Euch stoßen*, 46.
14. Luther, *D. Martin Luther's Werke*, vol. 25, 267.
15. Philip Melanchthon (1497–1560) was Luther's collaborator, who systematized Luther's ideas and is considered the intellectual leader and second founder of Lutheranism. And a bit of a scaredy-cat about bridges.

stays here because he looks at the stars; I stay here because I look at the bottom of my beer jar. The result is the same. He doesn't want to go home because he's afraid of the water—and I because I still want to have my drink."[16]

---

16. Kopp, "Horoskop und Genesis."

Chapter 2

Luther Was Upset About the Selling of Indulgences

Contrary to popular understanding, there is no such thing as an "indulgence for sin," a "get-out-of-purgatory-free card" or, more crassly, a go-and-sin-free card. Indulgences were and are granted to remit the *temporal* (earthly) punishment required for sin. In Catholic theology there are two consequences of sin: one, eternal punishment in hell, and two, earthly punishments for which one must make reparation. The eternal consequences of sin can be forgiven when sins committed after one's baptism are acknowledged in the sacrament of penance and reconciliation (confession) and one is restored to a state of grace.

But what about the temporal punishments due to sin? These must be expiated prior to death through pious acts of faith or after death through an indefinite time of purification (purgatory) so one is fit to enter God's presence. How can the penitent Christian know he or she has done enough good deeds to expiate one's temporal punishment for sin? By gaining an indulgence.

> There is one more method of expiation, and that is the gaining of indulgences. An indulgence is the remission of temporal punishment due to sins already forgiven. The merits gained by Christ

were enough to expiate all sins, and these merits, combined with the merits of Mary and the saints that were in excess of what they needed, form the Spiritual Treasury of the Church. It is from this treasury that the Church grants indulgences for the remission of temporal punishment, when a certain prayer or work is performed.[1]

As a Roman Catholic in good standing, Luther believed firmly that the church could grant indulgences. In other words, a priest was allowed to promise a reduction and shortening of the penance required for one's confessed sins or of time spent in purgatory to atone for one's sins not yet dealt with prior to death. As a priest, Luther issued indulgences in the confessional without hesitation and even collected financial donations for the building of St. Peter's Basilica in Rome. In fact, Luther was furious about the indulgence *trade*. His later anger about it set off an avalanche, which changed the world as we now know it in hindsight. But the simple view that Luther began the Reformation because he was against indulgences is, well, too simple, as we shall see.

What does the Bible say about indulgences?

With all the utmost esteem for my Catholic brothers and sisters: sorry—there's nothing there. Some of the first Christians in the Greek harbor city of Corinth were convinced of their blameless lifestyle, their exemplary conduct, and their good works. The apostle Paul knew, however, of the dark side of this church and wrote to them in 1 Corinthians 3:12–15:

> If anyone builds on this foundation using gold, silver, costly stones, wood, hay or straw, their work will be shown for what it is, because the Day will bring it to light. It will be revealed with fire, and the fire will test the quality of each person's work. If what has been built survives, the builder will receive a reward. If it is burned up, the builder will suffer loss but yet will be saved—even though only as one escaping through the flames.

---

1. "Temporal Punishment and Suffering," The Catholic Community Forum.

We do not know what exactly Paul meant by "fire"—was it an after-death-in-hell kind of fire or an apocalyptic catastrophe such as the end of the world? Or did he just—quite pragmatically—mean the next expected persecution of Christians in the Roman Empire? Historians and theologians are still arguing about it today. What we do know is that from these four verses by the apostle Paul, the church father Origen of Alexandria, in the third century, developed the idea of purgatory in the afterlife—an in-between stop on the way to paradise. In reality, this idea of a purification of the soul through fire is not found in either the Old or the New Testament.

Regarding the conquest and deportation of the Jews during the Babylonian exile in the sixth century BC, God said in Isaiah 48:10, "See, I have refined you . . . in the furnace of affliction." The apostle Peter wrote about the persecution of Christians by the mad Roman emperors in the first century: "These have come so that the proven genuineness of your faith—of greater worth than gold, which perishes even though refined by fire—may result in praise, glory and honor when Jesus Christ is revealed" (1 Peter 1:7). But a postmortem soul-purging by fire after death? Not a chance you'll find it in the Bible.

It didn't matter to Origen. He just estimated "one year in purgatory per day of sin on earth." Considering that in a lifetime, there are 365 days of sin times seventy-five years or so, it adds up. That's why the wish for a shortened time in purgatory was born—a very understandable wish, all things considered.

And what about forgiveness in the confessional process?

When I hurt or harm someone, when I disobey God's commands, when I sin and then repent, I must ask those I have wronged for forgiveness. Then, I hope, they will forgive me. Does the victim of my wrongdoing not want to forgive me or can they not forgive me? If the wrong cannot be righted on the human level, then I would at least like for *God* to forgive the sin. I confess it to him and ask for forgiveness. But how do I know that God really does that?

The Catholic answer is through someone who can, very officially "in the name of God," promise me a liberating absolution. *Ego te absolvo*, says the priest in the confessional—"I absolve you of your sins." Why can the priest grant this "absolution"? Because the Catholic Church understands itself as the administrator of the heavenly "treasury of grace." God's mercy and grace, the death of Jesus of Nazareth on the cross, the living sacrifice of the martyrs and saints—everything together is a type of divine treasure. So far, so good.

However, the Roman Catholic Church during Luther's time also understood itself as the administrator of *punishments*. In other words, it administered the requirements which one must bear, live up to, and fulfill in order to have forgiveness of the temporal consequences of sin. In the extreme medieval case, that could mean living one's life as a penitent, hermit, or monk, or participating as a "flagellant" in the more recently adopted (for Luther) Corpus Christi[2] procession where one was beaten on the shoulders and back with a small whip or lash. For aristocrats, knights, and the rich five hundred years before Luther, it meant taking part in the Crusades in the Middle East. However, the requirement was normally to make a pilgrimage to holy cities, to provide aid to the poor, to give money to the church, or to pray.

To be fair, we must admit that the forgiveness of sins in confession and absolution never was questioned by Luther. The priest's judgment call was only about the *earthly punishment* for one's sins, never eternal punishment. The degree of earthly punishment was negotiable in its severity and hardness in this world and its length in the next (that is, in purgatory). In short, the punishment of sins is first imposed and then alleviated by the confessor-priest. This mitigation is called "indulgence"—even today, by the way. In Roman Catholic canon law from 1983, canon 922 reads quite indisputably: "An indulgence is a remission before God of the

---

2. A celebration of the medieval Catholic Church involving processions and pageants in honor of the Holy Eucharist (hence *corpus christi*, "body of Christ"). Beginning in 1247 in Belgium, it took several decades to gain traction, but was universally celebrated by Catholics by 1325, just under two hundred years prior to Luther's protest in 1517.

temporal punishment due to sins whose guilt has already been forgiven."[3] As recently as December 2015 to November 2016, Roman Catholics around the world celebrated the Extraordinary Jubilee of Mercy proclaimed by Pope Francis I, a special feature of which was the chance to obtain one plenary indulgence a day or more than one partial indulgence. Such indulgences could be obtained for one's own benefit or for a soul in purgatory.[4]

So, why did Luther want to overturn this notion that has proven remarkably persistent in Roman Catholic tradition?

> "It pained me that my father and mother still lived! I would have liked to redeem them from the purgatorial fire with my masses and other splendid good works and prayers."

Let's be clear: for Luther, all of this was completely uncontentious until late summer 1517. During his stay in Rome in December 1510, he was very moved by the possibility of mitigating the punishment of sins for his deceased relatives. "It pained me that my father and mother still lived! I would have liked to redeem them from the purgatorial fire with my masses and other splendid good works and prayers,"[5] he remembered later, shaking his head. Luther loved to hear confessions as a priest and to forgive sins in the name of God. He was a responsive chaplain for people in moral dilemmas. It gave him great joy to comfort people, bring them back to the right path, and motivate them to spiritual exercises.

The only problem for Luther was that fewer people were coming to confession—or even to fast during the seven weeks before Easter in 1517. A certain Markus Menner happily showed Luther, the priest of the palace

---

3. This is in the recent valid Catholic world catechism under paragraph 1471.

4. Francis I, "Letter of His Holiness."

5. Krumbholz, *Euch stoßen*, 13.

church in Wittenberg, a piece of paper demonstrating why he no longer had to come to confession: "We proclaim to know by virtue of the
conferred authority upon us through this letter that Markus Menner is
absolved of the perpetrated homicide. We order each and every one that no
one—church official or layman—is to indict, judge, or damn him because
of the homicide."[6] This paper was signed by a Dominican monk named
Johann Tetzel, by order of Bishop Albrecht of Mainz and Magdeburg.

Luther was flabbergasted. In front of him stood a murderer who
thumbed his nose at the loving God! The dutiful Mr. Menner had paid
seven ducats[7] and even knew the bishop's price list partly by heart: robbery of a church, nine ducats; murder or manslaughter, seven; witchcraft,
six; adultery and child abuse, one per hit. But theft and smuggling—these
were cheap because one could donate a part of the goods or the dealer's
profits to the church. It was a commission to the pope so to say, on a
loosely negotiated basis.[8]

Martin Luther remembered that in 1506, Pope Julius II invented
the so-called indulgence of Peter, which empowered a priest to issue, in
addition to absolution, a mitigation of the temporal punishment of sins
in return for a donation to the building of St. Peter's Cathedral. But is
God's mercy then buyable? Well, sure! Public relations advisors of the
twenty-first century would have warned Julius that such a notion is the
proverbial slippery slope. But, hang on a minute (as Luther thought it
through)—then neither the *remorse* nor the *confession* nor the *absolution*
was the moving force in mitigation. It came merely after the confession
purely through the power of money. Luther himself, a dutiful Catholic
priest, had done it so since April 3, 1507!

---

6. Peltzer, *Das treffende Zitat*, 52.
7. Establishing a precise present-day value for the ducat is, well, hardly precise. We
   do know that less than twenty years previous, in 1499, noted Italian Leonardo da
   Vinci paid one ducat for a funeral, including the coffin, gravediggers, and a priest, as
   recorded in his notebook. Even allowing that funerals were more simple affairs back
   then, the price Mr. Menner paid to beat a murder rap was not cheap. See Abagond,
   "Money in Leonardo's Time."
8. Piltz, *Daher bin ich*, 78.

But we are ahead of ourselves. When the happy-to-build Pope Julius II died, his successor Leo X increased fundraising throughout Europe with the alteration that a generous donor could let their indulgence be registered in writing. With that development "indulgence letters" came into the world. And Luther didn't find them offensive. On the eve of All Saints' Day in 1514 (October 31 was definitely not yet Reformation Day), he said, "The intention, which the pope has through the giving of indulgences, is good!"[9] Two years later, on October 31, 1516, Luther was more distanced from it and more critical of indulgences: "In the real penance, the violation of justice must be atoned for; it prohibits therefore the indulgence and searches for the cross."[10]

And then this: in the summer of 1517, Luther rumbled through Germany on an extensive Visitation trip.[11] For two years, he was not only a lecturer of theology and a priest but also a district vicar and a supervisor of eleven monasteries, including Wittenberg. Everywhere he heard the same story about a Dominican monk, born in 1465 and educated in theology in Leipzig, who in 1509, as grand inquisitor in Poland, brought several heretics to be burned at the stake. His name was Johann Tetzel. Since then he had become an active seller of indulgences. Now he was reportedly on his way to the diocese of Magdeburg with a one-thousand-gulden annual salary and a large entourage. (He was earning ten times more than the mayor of Leipzig, a significant city, so business was good.)[12] Tetzel was later branded as not only a religious flimflam man but also an adulterer. Luther would much later report, in 1541, that Tetzel "had previously been rescued in Innsbruck by Duke Friedrich from a sack—for Maximilian had condemned him to be drowned in the river Inn (presumably on account of his great virtue)." The sarcasm of Luther's parenthetical comment provides a clear picture of what Luther thought of Tetzel. Whether the story

9. Ahrens, *Die Wittenbergisch Nachtigall*, 48.
10. Mayer, *Martin Luther*, 58.
11. Of course "Germany" in the modern sense didn't exist yet, but is used here for convenience. In military parlance, we might say Luther was out inspecting the troops.
12. Wolf, *Thesen*, 125.

of Tetzel's supposed dalliance is true or not is another matter. The main source for it is Luther himself, but almost four decades after the fact.[13]

Did Martin Luther and Johann Tetzel ever meet?

Unfortunately, no. But during his Visitation trip, Luther received written notes of Tetzel's sermons. What he read shocked him considerably: "Look at your mother! How she is tormented by the flames of purgatory! And that she suffers because of you! You could of course with your silver coins come to her rescue! But alas, woe to you, who despise God's mercy, which would indeed be so cheap to have!"[14]

> "As soon as a coin in the coffer rings
> the soul from purgatory springs!"
> —attributed to Johann Tetzel[15]

Tetzel's neat little rhetorical trick with the mother has a theological and a financial ulterior motive, of course. For over forty years, prayers, penance, and pilgrimages had been regarded as established Catholic practice to shorten purgatory for deceased relatives. Now, when one could take care of the whole thing with cash, Mr. Tetzel extended the list of sinful family members who could be covered endlessly. Indeed, please don't just think about the past, ladies and gentlemen! For the probable committed sins of the future, there was already a letter of indulgence here and now.

Luther himself records a supposed incident involving Tetzel and his trafficking in indulgences for sins not yet committed:

---

13. The story of Tetzel's near-death experience in a weighted sack appears in Luther's work *Wider Hans Worst* in 1541. That it is not attested earlier certainly seems suspect.
14. Peltzer, *Das treffende Zitat*, 54.
15. There is scholarly debate as to whether Tetzel actually coined (pun alert!) this phrase about coins in the coffer. Probably not, but it surely slipped his lips more than a time or two. That it shows up in Luther's theses twenty-seven and twenty-eight is evidence of its common use.

After Tetzel had received a substantial amount of money at Leipzig, a nobleman asked him if it were possible to receive a letter of indulgence for a future sin. Tetzel quickly answered in the affirmative, insisting, however, that the payment had to be made at once. This the nobleman did, receiving thereupon a letter and seal from Tetzel. When Tetzel left Leipzig the nobleman attacked him along the way, gave him a thorough beating, and sent him back empty-handed to Leipzig with the comment that this was the future sin which he had in mind. George, Duke of Saxony, at first was quite furious about this incident, but when he heard the whole story he let it go without punishing the nobleman.[16]

Luther's anger—later to become legendary—ostensibly wasn't ignited by Tetzel's rhetorical firecrackers, but rather because he undermined the entire salvation teaching of the church. "Tetzel's preaching is so coarse that one must intervene because he wrote and taught that the indulgence of the pope is already the reconciliation between God and man. On the other hand, he taught that the indulgence would be stronger and count as more because even when a man would not have remorse nor grief nor do penance, even so he, Tetzel, could forgive him!"

In thesis seventy-five Luther attacked indulgences with the most extreme example: "To consider papal indulgences so great that they could absolve a man even if he had done the impossible and had violated the mother of God is madness." Decades later he characterized Tetzel's beliefs in even more graphic terms:

It came to me how Tetzel had preached gruesome, abominable articles of which I will mention a few. Namely, he had such clemency and power from the pope that if one had deflowered or even impregnated the holy Virgin Mary, the mother of God, he could forgive it if that same one put in the chest what was required![17]

16. Luther, *Martin Luthers Sämtliche Schriften*, vol. 15, 446.
17. Krumbholz, *Euch stoßen*, 143.

Also:

> He would not trade places in heaven with St. Peter, for he had
> with indulgences saved more souls than St. Peter had with his
> sermons.[18]

That Tetzel ever made such a claim is hotly disputed by Catholic historians.

As Luther came back from his trip and was supposed to prepare the upcoming All Saints' Day celebration (together with a church service the evening before on October 31, 1517), he sat down and formulated his Ninety-Five Theses (topics for discussion) concerning the issues of confession and penance. Which began something far greater than Luther ever imagined—all because of indulgences.

---

18. Luther, *Wider Hans Worst.*

Chapter 3

Luther Planted an Apple Tree

"Even if I knew that tomorrow the world would go to pieces, I would still plant my apple tree."

Vintage Luther, right?

No, unfortunately a myth, but a popular one at least!

We don't want to eliminate the possibility that he was just helping his wife, Katharina, with planting fruit trees in the garden. However, on October 5, 1944, a clergyman named Karl Lotz from Hesse wrote this famous saying on his mechanical typewriter in a newsletter to friends from the Confessing Church. The Confessing Church was a movement of German Christians who resisted the co-opting of the German Protestant church by the Nazi-approved German Christians movement. In May 1934 the Confessing Church adopted the Barmen Declaration (named after the city in which they met) in which they stood against Adolf Hitler's Nazi ideology and the subordination of the church to the state. Those who signed the declaration and their friends lived in danger throughout the war as Germany was ruled by the terror of the SS and Gestapo.

It is quite remarkable, then, that Mr. Lotz had the courage not only to duplicate and send such a letter, which pitted him against the ruthless power of the Nazi state, but also to choose these words: "Please do not let yourself be annoyed by my writing given the tense state of our people. We must look to the words of Luther: 'If the world goes under tomorrow . . .'"[1]

Seven months later, of course, the world did go under—the German world anyways, on May 8, 1945, with the death of Hitler and Germany's surrender.

Where did Karl Lotz get the idea that this was a saying of Luther? Neither in the collection of Luther's seven thousand table talks edited by Ernst Kroker in 1903 nor in the Weimar edition of Luther's complete works from 1883 is the saying—or any saying—about an apple tree to be found. Perhaps the courageous resistance preacher unconsciously mixed up Martin Luther with the Württemberg preacher Johann Albrecht Bengel (1687–1752). Based on chapter 20 of the New Testament book of Revelation, Bengel believed in the beginning of a two-thousand-year countdown until the visible second coming of Jesus Christ to earth and the end of the world. The start of the countdown was to be June 18, 1836.

Bengel died in 1752 but his supporters found one thousand years times two just too many times too long, so they spread the notion that the date *itself* was the calculated second coming of Jesus. The Napoleonic Wars and a series of bad harvests in Württemberg since 1817 appeared to confirm to many that the end times had arrived. It should also be noted that there was a growing dissatisfaction with the regional church, so much so that some Pietists felt compelled to emigrate to Russia, for example. Asked where all of these little biblical number games came into play, the immigrants replied, "And if we had known, that tomorrow the world goes under . . ."

So perhaps the courageous pastor Lotz drew upon his knowledge of German theologians (slightly mixed together) to come up with an inspiring quote, but didn't get it quite right. No matter—never let the facts get in the way of a good quote! Over the years, the apple tree and Luther continue to be passed on in the popular imagination.

The noted German poet Gottfried Benn once again rooted the apple tree tightly in Luther's spiritual possession in a poem from 1950:

---

1. Schloemann, *Luthers Apfelbäumchen?*, 28.

> What did Luther mean with the apple tree?
> It's the same to me. The downfall is a dream.
> I stand here in my apple garden
> And can expect the downfall confidently.
> I am in God, who is outside of the world
> still holding some trump card in his hand.[2]

In the age of the Internet, Luther's apple tree has taken on a curious life of evolving misattribution. It's easy enough to find numerous memes with this inspiring quote (often overlaid on sunny green fields with a hopeful apple tree in the foreground). Surprisingly, one will also find it attributed to the Rev. Dr. Martin Luther King Jr. Most likely Dr. King used this quote in his speeches, perhaps optimistically expecting his audience to be familiar with the source, perhaps based on the fact that he himself bore the name of the great reformer. Evidently, some listeners didn't make the connection.

Ironically, it was not a believer in Luther's Christian hope that would find a use for the saying, but the secularist physicist, television celebrity, and scientific journalist Hoimar von Ditfurth. In his book, he denounced the technological, economical, and liberal exploitation of natural resources and predicted the world's imminent environmental collapse—a sort of secular second coming with no deity involved.

He titled his best seller *Let Us Then Plant an Apple Tree. It Is Time.*

Of course, that book was written "way back" in 1985. No end of the world yet. Evidently, it still isn't time.

---

2. In a letter to Thilo Koch on May 26, 1950, in Benn, *Ausgewählte Briefe*, 191.

Chapter 4

Luther Was a Poor Farmer's Son

It makes for a nice story arc—a poor son of the soil struggles against the odds and by sheer force of talent achieves fame and success, all the while his doting parents are smiling broadly for the neighbors and kin. Definitely a familiar movie trope. Except in Luther's cause, this is not exactly how the story unfolded.

Luther said himself, "My father, grandfather, and ancestors were real peasants. Then, my father moved to Mansfeld and became a miner."[1] First farmer, then miner? Luther's family came from Möhra, a village on the south-facing slope of the Thuringian Forest in what is now the east side of central Germany.[2] Supposedly Martin was born as the first of eight children in Eisleben on November 10, 1483.

Did his father, Hans, arrive there as a poor farmer? No, not likely. One year after Martin's birth, the young family moved to Mansfeld and could afford to buy the house in which they lived. To say he was a "miner" in slate flooring in the county of Mansfeld is an understatement. Hans Luther leased a small company, which conducted copper mining.

---

1. Süßenguth, *Aus einem traurigen Arsch*, 16.
2. Oddly enough, this area would figure prominently in future history. The Wartburg, the castle where Luther took refuge for nearly a year, stands in Thuringia. The nearby town of Weimar became the ill-fated capital of the Weimar Republic after World War I.

Because Hans lived in the township of Eisleben, his two sons Martin and Jacob were able to study at school, and the three daughters Margarethe, Elisabeth, and Dorothea could be given a dowry when they married. This does not suggest a proletarian life as a working-class peasant. Because we have a portrait of Hans and his wife painted by the expensive artist Lucas Cranach the Elder in 1527–1528, it also cannot be accepted uncritically that they were peasants. The squalor of Martin Luther's ancestry—fondly highlighted during his four-hundredth birthday celebration in East Germany in 1983—was due to the fact that his parents lived very frugally in order to earn interest and income from their business capital. That inconvenient capitalistic fact, of course, would have been at odds with the East German communist view.

> "The man is supposed to earn money; the woman, however,
> is supposed to save it. . . . For the saved penny is better
> than the earned. So, frugality is the best type of earning."

"The man is supposed to earn money; the woman, however, is supposed to save it. In this way, the woman can make the man rich, not the man the woman. For the saved penny is better than the earned. So, frugality is the best type of earning."[3] This advice was given to a couple and probably came from childhood experiences. When Martin became a professor at the University of Wittenberg in 1512, his father Hans was still a partner in eight mines and three copper mills. At his death in 1530, Hans left his son an inheritance of 15,500 gulden.[4]

Luther's great appreciation of social responsibility and generous Christian love, his generous lifelong donations, and his almsgiving did not come from some naive or pious ideal of poverty. "If a Christian is supposed

---

3. Luther, *Tischreden*, 289.
4. Wolf, *Thesen*, 132.

to give, he must first have something to give. Whoever has nothing has nothing to give. And if he is supposed to give something tomorrow and the next day, he cannot give away everything today. Our Lord Christ does not desire that I give my possessions to the beggar, and the beggar to the Lord. Instead, I should look after his destitute needs and help him as much as I can, so that the poor eat with me and not I with the poor."[5]

It is a pity that we cannot ask him whether he was referring just to families and private property or also to the church as an institution. When Jorge Bergoglio, also known as Pope Francis, was appointed as pope in March 2013, he urged for a poor church near the poor and proceeded with a good example. He visited the Middle Eastern refugees on the Italian island of Lampedusa, the detainees in prison, and the destitute people living in the notorious favela slums in Rio de Janeiro. They were thankful for so much attention and appreciation but also made it clear that they definitely did not want a *poor* church! The Catholic Dalits in India, who are "untouchables" of the lowest caste, said at the German Catholic Congress in Regensburg in May 2014 that only a wealthy church could give donations and microcredit, run kindergartens, and build schools, hospitals, and retirement homes.

So, no, Luther was in reality from a solidly middle-class background yet understood that the point of having money was not to have it, but to use it for the benefit of others. One wonders what the rigorously parsimonious Hans Luther would have thought of that.

---

5. Luther, *D. Martin Luther's Werke*, vol. 52, 384.

Chapter 5

Luther Was a Boozer

Despite the popular image of Luther as a jolly monk knocking back steins of home brew, Luther wasn't a boozer. While Luther was a drinker (and who wasn't in the sixteenth century?), he always condemned drunkenness. Why, then, in the popular imagination at least, is Luther thought to be a vigorous elbow-bender who extolled a hearty ale or boisterous beer as the gift of God? Stories and quotes about Luther and beer, both real and fictitious, are only an Internet search away. Ponder which of the following are actual quotes from Luther:

1. "Whoever drinks beer, he is quick to sleep; whoever sleeps long does not sin; whoever does not sin enters Heaven! Thus, let us drink beer!"
2. "Beer is proof that God loves us and wants us to be happy."
3. "If you are tired and downhearted, take a drink; but this does not mean being a pig and doing nothing but gorging and swilling."

Number one is a widely quoted "quote" of Luther's, according to the Internet at least, but seems to have appeared suddenly in 2007 on a blog. Whether it has anything to do with Luther is disputed.

Number two is a ringer—history lovers will immediately recognize the genial wit of Ben Franklin's famous quote.

Number three—here is an actual Luther quote from a sermon preached on May 18, 1539. Hardly a ringing endorsement of wild debauchery. Luther the real drinker and Luther the drinker of legend seem to actually have little resemblance.

Luther knew from his time in Erfurt and later in the Augustine monastery in Wittenberg that self-imposed abstention could sometimes be sensible and advisable, but in the end it only intensified the longing. Generally speaking, trying to keep a diet means thinking of food more than usual. The more a person consciously tries to stay awake, the more they will eagerly want to go to sleep. Whoever is not allowed to have sex will want it all the more. Luther knew from his own experience that we cannot always overcome our inner desires and reach our good resolutions. As someone who heard the confessions of thousands of people seeking advice, he must have been all too familiar with the fact that people can succumb to their temptations, and the more often they do, the more often they simply let themselves go or give up.

Such experiences create a bad conscience and lead to disappointment with one's self. Little by little, self-esteem evaporates, and one loses the feeling of self-worth. This effect, and not alcohol itself, Luther named the "work of the devil" or "of the devil's mockery." Thus he counseled his roommate, Jerome Weller, who was plagued by self-doubt and melancholy:

> Whenever the devil plagues you with such thoughts, look to converse with people, drink more, joke more, amuse yourself, and search for cheerful things! In such cases, one must drink, play, and jest more abundantly and thus commit a sin against the devil's hate and scorn. In this we should never give him the space to weigh down our conscience over such minor things. When we worry too much about not sinning, we will be overcome by the devil. Thus, when the devil says: "Don't drink," answer him so: "Just for this reason, now all the more, I will drink because you hinder me!" We must always do the opposite of what the devil forbids.[1]

---

1. Bernhard, *Martin Luther Hausbuch*, 57.

Does the devil disguise himself as a moralist and guardian of virtue to bring the weak and seducible person of integrity down all the deeper? It is a thought that not everyone can comprehend, especially when Luther used the example of alcohol. Luther's contemporaries who didn't wish to follow this frame of mind were outraged by his perceived praise of tippling, just as some Christian traditions and all Mormon and Muslim groups (and the occasional health freak) are also hypervigilant today. On the other hand, there are those who misunderstand him when they, in the truest sense of the word *complacent*, quote from Luther's table talks: "Tomorrow I must give a lecture about Noah's drunkenness. Therefore, this evening I will drink bountifully, so that I can speak as an expert on this wicked matter."[2] Or from letters to Katharina, whilst traveling: "I gourmandize like a Bohemian and booze like a German."[3]

"Tomorrow I must give a lecture about Noah's drunkenness. Therefore, this evening I will drink bountifully, so that I can speak as an expert on this wicked matter."

When Bishop Dantiscus, the Polish Catholic critic of the Reformation, arrived in Wittenberg in 1523, he looked down his nose at Luther, saying, "Apart from coarse jokes and biting remarks against the pope, emperor, and some princes, he has produced nothing of consideration." However, Dantiscus was pleasantly touched by Luther's hospitality and drinking habitudes, stating, "We drank wine and beer in good spirit, as it is custom there. Luther seems in this respect to be a good fellow, as one says in German."[4]

Now one could infer from a gastro-psychological point of view that the youthful, super-abstinent monk Martin may have fallen into the

---

2. Zitelmann, *Ich, Martin Luther*, 57.
3. Joestel, *Thesentür und Tintenfaß*, 26.
4. Hürlimann, *Martin Luther*, 69.

other extreme of being overly self-indulgent. This would have quenched the need to catch up on all those lost pints from his monastery days—although there was a brewery in the monastery in Erfurt. Some quotes seem even to reinforce this theory: "Can the Lord God give me this: I have crucified and tortured the body for a good twenty years by holding masses, thus he can grant me this, that I occasionally take a good drink to bring him honor. May God give the world what it wants."[5]

Of course the world laid it out as it wanted. From April 24 to October 4, 1530, Luther lived in the Coburg Fortress in Franconia. He wanted to be far away but close to what was happening, especially to keep a watch on developments at the Diet of Augsburg. He is supposed to have consumed twelve hundred liters of wine during his stay in the castle—according to the Catholic attendees at the diet. This, of course, is an all too transparent rumor: consuming six liters of wine per day, Luther would hardly have been able to write "An Open Letter on Translating" in Coburg and prepare his lectures on Galatians for the following summer semester. Much less even stand upright.

His puffy, doughy face provided a good point of attack for some opponents. The papal nuncio (or representative) Peter Paul Vergerius visited Luther in Wittenberg in November 1535 and wrote to Pope Paul III, "He has a seemingly fat face; indeed, he wills himself to give an ailing expression. He has widely torn eyes, and the longer I looked at them, the more it occurred to me how they looked like the eyes of one who is possessed."[6] Not that the emissary of the pope would have been biased.

That the famous and adored university professor Dr. Luther "shaved at most twice a week"[7] guaranteed stubble on his chin and cheeks. A scruffy guy with beery breath? Admittedly, as the freshly married Katharina von Bora entered the bachelors' apartment in the former monastery in Wittenberg in 1525, where her Martin had lived with the apparently idle servant Wolf Seeberger since 1511, "the bedroom of the doctor stank of a

---

5. Joestel, *Legenden um Luther*, 69.
6. Bernhard, *Martin Luther Hausbuch*, 584.
7. Piltz, *Daher bin ich*, 7.

doghouse. The year-old bedstraw, which hadn't been replaced, rotted in front of him," and the only excuse that the sheepish husband offered was, "I slave away the day, then fall into my bed and didn't know anything about it."[8] So, characterizing Luther (in the modern vernacular) as a beer-belching frat boy in need of a bath would not have seemed far off the mark were we transported back in time.

Not that Wittenberg was a model community to begin with. The university rector, Christoph von Scheurl, described the nearly two thousand residents of Wittenberg as "crude, gluttonous and sottish."[9] And Luther himself sneered, "The people of Wittenberg are on the border of civilization. Pushed a little further, they would fall into barbarism."[10]

So, was he a somewhat confused, occasionally drunken professor before his marriage?

Not at all. First of all because Luther had come to know the devastating consequences of alcoholism when he was an overseer of eleven monasteries and as a chaplain to the palace church in Wittenberg. He ranted from the pulpit against excess and recommended modest pleasure as a good balance between asceticism and overindulgence. "It is granted to you and every man through God that you do not only eat and drink to your essential needs, but rather to pleasure and joy and all good things. But with this you shall not allow yourself to be satisfied—unless you want to be such a pig and a disgusting creature, as if you were merely born for consuming beer and wine!"[11]

Perhaps it was the somewhat contradictory lifestyle of Luther that confuses more modern commentators. On the one hand, Luther himself had arranged for his wife, Katharina, to buy the brewing rights from the monastery in Wittenberg, and on her documented shopping list we find hops, malt, and barley. On the other hand, we have the more cautious Luther thundering, "Whoever invented brewing was an evil for Germany!"[12]

---

8. Ibid., 128.
9. Krumbholz, *Euch stoßen*, 242.
10. Ibid.
11. Schorlemmer, *Hier stehe ich*, 149.
12. Brüllmann, *Lexikon der treffenden Martin-Luther-Zitate*, 25.

Luther even wished that alcohol production and consumption would be more strongly regulated by law and that alcohol abuse would be made a punishable offense. Since he had not had any success with the nobles or ruling powers—"I've recently given a hard and harsh sermon against boozing, but it was no use"[13]—he had the sarcastic idea to absurdly turn around the ban: "When I come again to the princes, then I will request nothing else than that he demand his subjects and courtiers everywhere that they get quite drunk and fuddled, or otherwise suffer a harsher punishment. Perhaps when something is forbidden, they will want to do the opposite."[14]

When such ironical statements are read centuries later, the occasion, as well as the relevant historical context, can indeed get lost and as a result be turned upside down. As if Luther had seriously said that boozing is sensible and abstinence is crazy—he didn't!

Ironically (that word again!), the warmhearted, well-behaved, highly sensitive, pious German poet and journalist Matthias Claudius (1740–1815) wrote an article in his newspaper, *Der Wandsbecker Bothe* (1775), with an erroneous quote of Luther's: "Whoever doesn't love wine, woman and song, he shall remain a fool his whole life long."[15] The simple couplet probably originated from Claudius's contemporary and fellow journalist Johann Heinrich Voss.[16] It was Luther, however, dead for more than two centuries, who would get the credit for the ribaldry.

Against the suspicion that Luther was an alcoholic, there are at least three pieces of evidence: his admirable discipline, his incredible workload (not even counting the Herculean task of his Bible translation), and his twenty-one-year intact marriage and family life along with the high esteem of his relatives.

And finally, an unfortunate detail: Luther had gallstones or kidney stones, which in February 1537 led to an eight-day urinary retention.

---

13. Maess, *Dem Luther aufs Maul geschaut*, 77.
14. Brüllmann, *Lexikon der treffenden Martin-Luther-Zitate*, 78.
15. Luther, *Legenden um Luther*, 22.
16. Mieder, "Ist das jetzt spruchreif?"

Under agony he cried, "If there was only a Turk here to slaughter me! Meanwhile, I, with a strong and healthy body, must perish in my own water!"[17] Short and simple: urination hurt too badly to even enjoy the thought of drinking.

17. Wolf, *Luther*, 128.

Chapter 6

Luther Translated the First German Bible

As with our other Luther myths, a simple "no" may again suffice. A certain Mister Ulfilas did that. He lived between AD 311 and 383 in what is today northern Bulgaria and belonged to the Goths, an East Germanic people group. One can, of course, argue whether it was really "German" that he wrote. Want to evaluate the evidence? The Lord's Prayer by Ulfilas begins as follows:

> *Atta unsar*
> *þu in himimam*
> *weihnai namo þein*
> *qimai þiudinassus þeins*
> *Warpai will ja þeins*
> *swe in himima*
> *ja ana arþei.*

Not really much like modern German or even Luther's older German for that matter, so score one for the anti-Ulfilas viewpoint. The good missionary Ulfilas also only translated those parts of the Bible that he held to be compatible with the Goths. For example, he found the Old Testament unsuitable for the always-eager-for-war Germanic tribe due to the considerable amount of violence it contains—which seems in hindsight like an astute choice.

But twelve hundred years later—during Luther's time—seventy-two partial German translations of the Bible had *already* been produced.[1] Their translators remained, for safety's sake, anonymous. John Wycliffe in England, for example, who compiled an English translation of the Bible, died very naturally of a stroke in 1384, but was labeled a heretic during the Council of Constance in 1415. Whereupon his bones were unearthed and burned in 1428, forty-four years after his death, something of little consequence to Wycliffe himself. Such a thing could have also taken place in the German dioceses *before* a translator's untimely death. Therefore, the conventional wisdom was: no names, please, to anyone.

Furthermore, the available German translations of parts of the Bible had two serious flaws. One, they were not translated from the oldest attainable Greek and Hebrew texts but instead relied only on the Latin text, tracing its lineage to St. Jerome in the late fourth century. And two, they were so literally translated from the Latin that the meaning in German remained nearly incomprehensible. "Garbled, jumbled, and muddled" is one description. They also didn't achieve large print runs: "Thirty years ago no one read the Bible," Luther recalled in 1538. "It was as good as completely unknown. When I was twenty years old, I had never seen one."[2]

For us today, such ignorance is unheard of in Christian families. However, pious Christian parents in the 1500s, like Martin's, didn't read Bible stories to their children. Rather, they turned to legends of the saints. Songs to Mary, blessings, liturgical phrases from the Mass, which one could—in accordance with the magical worldview of the time—recite in an oracular manner, were popular. To us today it seems obvious that a priest or minister should be, first of all, a Bible expert. Not back then: Martin Luther was ordained as a priest on April 3, 1507, celebrated his first Mass on May 2, and *after that* began his studies in theology!

---

1. Kleinschmidt, *Martin Luther*, 74.
2. Zitelmann, *"Widerrufen kann ich nicht,"* 21.

So why did he translate the Bible at all?

Ostensibly, one could say "because of boredom." After his orchestrated "kidnapping" on May 4, 1521, he lived under a false name in two small chambers in the Wartburg castle and was supposed to sit still until times got better. But being Luther, it was not to be.

Actually, he had thought about the idea much longer. If only "the mother in the home, the children on the street, and the ordinary man"[3] could read those words of Jesus and the letters of Paul, which had grabbed and freed him! If only each and every person could verify whether the princes and bishops really spoke in God's name or merely assumed a mantle of speaking in God's name. If "we could believe that God speaks to us in his Holy Word, then we would more eagerly read it and would be certain that here our happiness will be forged!"[4]

> "[If] we could believe that God speaks to us in his Holy Word, then we would more eagerly read it and would be certain that here our happiness will be forged!"

Certainly not only was "the missionary in Luther's heart" chomping at the bit but the dedicated professor of theology also wanted some work. In 1519 the world-famous scholar Erasmus of Rotterdam published an edition of the New Testament in the original Greek. Now one could check and compare the original text with the Vulgate, which was the Latin Bible quoted in the Catholic Mass. Philip Melanchthon brought these two "Bibles"—a New Testament in Greek and one in Latin—to his friend in the Wartburg castle and commented, "I hope we will give our Germany a better one than the Latin scholars had. This is a great work and worthy to be done."[5] Luther was certainly motivated by his love

---

3. Wolf, *Thesen*, 28.
4. Mayer, *Martin Luther*, 110.
5. Köthe, *Martin Luther und Luthergedenkstätten*, 104.

of God's Word. A little rebelliousness and a desire to provoke were also motives, since from where or whom did Luther in fact have the right to edit the Holy Scripture? From no one, of course. "Luther worked without authority," observed an astonished Gotthold Lessing (1729–1781), "against the church's presumed truth that it was better that the Bible isn't read by common men."[6]

And how did he do it then? Like a madman. From December 1521 to February 1522, in just eleven weeks, in fact, Luther translated daily ten to twelve pages of the New Testament. In doing so he had to leave gaps open: "It happened often that we searched and enquired after one single word for two or three or four weeks at a stretch. However, we didn't find it. Sometimes we could hardly finish three lines in four days."[7]

To understand the sheer ingenuity of his accomplishment, one must also consider the history of the New Testament itself. Jesus didn't leave behind a single written line from his own hand (which may surprise some). He most likely spoke Aramaic, although we can infer that he also probably knew and spoke both Hebrew and Greek on occasion. (After all, Palestine had been a crossroads of many cultures for hundreds of years, not some bumpkin backwater.) His words were translated in various missionary situations initially by at least seventy disciples (Luke 10:1) and were retold orally later on by dozens, even hundreds (Acts 1:15; 2:41). Some of the twelve disciples of Jesus, the apostles, noted and translated the events from memory, in some books using good Greek (Luke) and in others using plainer Greek (Peter and Mark). For a period of at least three hundred years, various gospels, letters, stories of Jesus, acts of martyrs, and legends of saints circulated around the Mediterranean world. Which groups of Christians held which texts varied by region. But the fastest spreading of Christianity—the most "fruitful" decades of mission—occurred without a complete set of New Testament writings being universally available.

Even today, nobody possesses the original manuscripts of the Bible authors. The oldest Christian Bible in Greek, including the oldest complete

---

New Testament, was discovered by the Leipzig researcher Constantin von Tischendorf in 1844 in Saint Catherine's Monastery on Mount Sinai. This aptly named Codex Sinaiticus comes from around AD 350 and is the oldest substantial book to survive from antiquity.[8]

That is not to say, however, that we don't have substantive portions of the New Testament from earlier times. There are also over 130 papyrus fragments from the late first to mid third century that have been discovered, some within the last few years. New Testament scholar Dan Wallace estimates that the first- and second-century fragments alone contain over 43 percent of the New Testament.[9] In short, there was never an original text of the New Testament known and used by every Christian everywhere. Martin Luther knew that. We have copies of copies, and some bits are translations of translations.[10] Martin Luther knew that as well. And it wasn't a problem.

This fact alone moved Martin Luther to an attitude of reverence and awe! That the living God didn't just let his living Word fall from the sky but instead entrusted it to the mouths and hands of humans provoked a grateful admiration in Luther. He felt a high regard for the Holy Scriptures. At the same time, however, his knowledge of languages gave him great freedom. Because the most literal translation is not always the most meaningful, he interpreted away cheerfully. To name one example: one of the core verses of the Reformation, the heart of the gospel faith, is Romans 3:28, which Luther translated like this: "Therefore, we hold

---

8. "As it survives today, Codex Sinaiticus comprises just over 400 large leaves of prepared animal skin. . . . On these parchment leaves is written around half of the Old Testament and Apocrypha (the Septuagint), the whole of the New Testament, and two early Christian texts not found in modern Bibles." See "Content," The Codex Sinaiticus Project.

9. Wallace, "Earliest Manuscript of the New Testament Discovered?"

10. That is not to say that we don't know what the writers of the New Testament really said. "We have over 5,700 Greek manuscripts representing all, or part, of the NT. By examining these manuscripts, over 99 percent of the original text can be reconstructed beyond reasonable doubt. We also discover that no Christian doctrine or ethic depends solely on one of the doubted texts. These facts do not prove that the NT is true, but it does mean we know what the original writers wrote." Stetzer, "A Closer Look."

that man is justified without the works of the law, alone through faith."
Wonderful truth. Except the word "alone" is nowhere to be found in
Greek text—as Luther himself admitted!

> So, I knew very well that the word "alone" was not to be found
> in Greek, nor in Latin. It is true: the four letters "sola" are not to
> be found! Letters, at which the papal donkeys' heads are gazing
> like a cow at a new gate. I am, however, so confidently moved not
> only by the idiosyncrasy of the languages that I put in "alone" but
> also by the text and meaning of Paul demanding it and compel-
> ling me with violence![11]

After Luther's return to Wittenberg, the meticulous double-checker
Philip Melanchthon strove to have the most possible faithfulness to the
text when it came to the issue of "poetic freedom." Melanchthon, the
Greek expert, argued with his friend Luther over each word in the translation through March and April 1522. In order not to offend him personally, Melanchthon acknowledged, "You should know, Martinus, for me,
it's just about the Greek!" To which Luther responded, "For me, it's just
about the German!"[12]

For Lucas Cranach the Elder (1472–1553), the famous artist in Wittenberg right next door to Luther, so to speak, it was just about the visuals.
He prepared woodcarvings and vignettes to illustrate the printed translation. The printer, Melchior Lotter, typeset the translation and printed
three thousand copies for the first edition. In September 1522, *Das Newe
Testament Deutzch* (The German New Testament) was finally released. It
cost 1.50 gulden, which was quite expensive for the time, approximately
the annual salary of a housemaid. Nonetheless, in three months all the
"September Testaments" were sold out, and the fortunate Melchior Lotter
had to reprint seventeen more editions in the following twelve years.

---

11. Hörster, *Markenzeichen bibeltreu*, 31.
12. Friedrich and Schank, *Die besten Anekdoten*, 337.

Chapter 7

Luther Ate While Preaching

One would not be blamed for thinking that the words "table talk" and "Martin Luther" surely must mean listening to sermons between snacks. Because it's difficult to understand people who talk while they eat, let's listen again more closely.

Luther lived with his wife in the former Black Abbey of the Augustine monks from 1525 onward. Later on, he lived there along with his six children (four of whom survived to adulthood), a son of his brother, Jacob Luther, and Katharina von Bora's orphaned nephew, Fabian. From 1530 onward, the orphaned nieces and nephews of two of Martin's late sisters lived in the house as well. In addition, there was a revolving number of foster children; "Auntie Lehne," the treasured foster mother and maid; Wolf Seeberger, the lethargic servant; and "a mix of young students and girls, from widows, old women, and celibate boys; therefore there is a lot of unrest there,"[1] warned a royal supporter, Prince George III of Anhalt-Dessau, when he was asked whether one could stay overnight in Luther's house. No, not recommended. Luther's house was as busy as a pigeon coop. Which begs the obvious question: Why was that?

When Frederick the Wise, prince of Saxony, founded the University

---

1. Piltz, *Daher bin ich*, 132.

of Wittenberg in 1502, he specified in the monastery agreement that the professors had to teach free of charge because they were monks who ate and slept in the monastery—a nonpaying gig, in other words. As a result of the Reformation, the Catholic monasteries were changed into "sacred" student dorms so it was no longer the responsibility of Prince Frederick to provide for basic necessities, the most important of which was food. Therefore, the students *and* lecturers were happy that there was a daily lunch for everyone at mother Katharina Luther's table, a sort of community kitchen for the university.

Katharina, the ex-nun, attracted several women to Wittenberg who had followed her example and abandoned their monasteries. George, Duke of Saxony, complained about this in a letter to Martin Luther: "You have offered asylum in Wittenberg so that all monks and nuns can find refuge with you, as if Wittenberg were a *ganerben*[2] of all the rebels in the country."[3] By the way, the Luthers also took in other religious sectarians and therefore harbored political rebels. The crueler the Inquisition raged at the "heretical" Lutherans in Catholic areas of Europe, the more persecuted believers from Austria, Switzerland, Hungary, Bohemia, and Denmark came knocking at the door in Wittenberg.

As many as forty people ate at the table, predominantly intellectuals of all ages (which surely must have allowed for some interesting conversations). "Even when Dr. Luther occasionally observed his old familiar habit of monastic silence during the meal, and when no word was spoken at the table, he still talked now and then, very amusingly and jokingly," the student Johannes Mathesius remembered.[4]

"Now and then amusingly?" That is very modestly formulated to describe a person such as Luther. Luther's vivid examples, his comparisons and figures of speech, and his wise, but often vulgar, sayings made the rounds of the Wittenberg bars (and even five hundred years later, these are

---

2. A house owned jointly by heirs who shared rights to a property. Today we might say that Luther was being accused of running a commune of questionable character.
3. Landgraf, *Martin Luther*, 106.
4. Mayer, *Martin Luther*, 249.

still, for some, the only things they know about Luther). Some examples (and remember I've already said Luther could be vulgar):

"Out of a sad ass comes no happy fart."[5]

"Beware of cats that lick in the front and scratch in the back."[6]

"Rule by women doesn't have a happy ending."[7]

Luther's students noted down what their professor spouted privately and spontaneously, took these bon mots to the local printer, and from these sayings made cards, leaflets, and flyers. The small profit from the sale of these personal tidbits all went to the students, not the originator.

In 1531, the fifty-one-year-old Austrian clergyman Konrad Cordatus requested Luther's permission to regularly take notes of everything he said while dining. He called the casual quotes "table talks." That label is not totally accurate since Cordatus gives us what seem to be prepared and drafted speeches at the table. Was Cordatus thinking already as a church historian? Or was he just a fan? Or did he simply want to make himself useful because he was living off Luther? It's hard to tell.

From 1537 on, the twenty-eight-year-old theology student and later court chaplain in Weimar, Johannes Aurifaber, resumed the tradition of keeping notes until Luther's death in 1546. In 1566, he released a book with the wonderful title *Table Talks or Colloquia of Dr. Martin Luther, as He Held over Many Years Toward Learned People, as Well as Foreign Guests, and His Companions at the Table.* Was the diligent Mr. Aurifaber then an early modern Dictaphone, through whose recordings we can listen to the Reformation live? Unfortunately, not.

There were other distinguished "secretaries" around the prominent preacher. Anton Lauterbach, Dietrich Medler, Ludwig Rabe, Hieronymus

---

5. Süßenguth, *Aus einem traurigen Arsch*, 1.
6. Wolf, *Luther*, 86.
7. Ibid., 85.

Weller—these men all discussed, compared, edited, and revised the texts, especially after Luther died and the spontaneous events and causes of the talks faded in memory or were forgotten. Already within twenty years after his death, Luther's *Table Talks* were the result of editorial revision and had been more or less tweaked.

What's more, the Latin language in the sixteenth century had approximately the same function as English nowadays: a transnational way of communication, a lingua franca of the educated class. Luther certainly didn't speak or preach Latin continuously, but his table talks were interspersed with Latin terms, as well as borrowed words from Latin and Latin-German word combinations.

Luther's table talks are, then, translations. The cowriter, Veit Dietrich, noted, "*Quando tentaris tristitia aut desparatione aut alio dolore conscientiae, tunc ede, bibe quaere colloquia, si potes te cogitatione puellae recreare, facito.*" Translated by the classicist Walter Jens, this says: "If you are troubled by sadness or despair or another pain of the conscience—then eat, drink, and search for sociable conversations. If you can please yourself with the thoughts of a girl—then simply do it!"[8]

Johannes Aurifaber repeated this text in 1566 with a definite spin: "Whoever is plagued by sadness, despair or heartache and has a worm in their conscience, *seek firstly the comfort of the Word of God*. Afterward, eat and drink and seek companionship and conversation *of blessed and Christian people*, in this way one will become better."[9] Oh really? He just came up with the "comfort of the Word of God" and romantic fantasies morphed into "blessed Christian people"?

But without the Latin sprinklings we would hardly understand the real Luther quotes. Take for example this saying: "I think that if God had offered that a woman is supposed to admit who came there and in turn a man which one came in summa if it were reverse I think that one would have loudly groaned after the marriage."[10]

---

8. Henkys, *Luthers Tischreden*, 14.
9. Ibid.
10. Ibid., 144, 285.

Makes sense, right? If one tries to translate the meaning, Luther is roughly saying: "Had God required that a woman had to give herself away to a perfect stranger and vice versa, each man for each woman, then people would eagerly wish for marriage, I believe." Well, that was Luther's opinion. Even made more plain, it doesn't really make a lot of sense.

Also, to understand the noted table talks in German, one needs to read the translation transcriptions. That is not a disadvantage. Luther's delightful way with words still works in German and in English as well:

> If we did what we should,
> and didn't do what we want,
> then we would have what we are supposed to have.
> But now we do what we want,
> and not what we should;
> we should resist that which we don't want.[11]

In my opinion, well put.

Not until 1903 did a theologian by the name of Ernst Kroker begin to critically document Luther's table talks by origin, authenticity, translation, and editorial work; and he collected them in 1921 into six volumes to be added to the 1883 Weimar edition of Luther's works. More than seven thousand table talks were passed down between 1531 and 1546. That is 467 per year, or nine table talks per week! In the Black Abbey in Wittenberg overseen by Katharina and Martin, there was, however, at most only one warm meal per day between 5 and 6 p.m. If Luther is supposed to have given more than one talk per day, then perhaps he also spoke twice a week with a cold meal.

No matter—it is a prodigious collection of sayings with or without actual food. The point is, however, that Luther didn't preach while he ate. And neither should any preacher. So help them God.

---

11. Wolf, *Eine Frage noch*, 26.

Chapter 8

Luther Intended to Establish an Independent Church

So far we've been dipping our feet into the shallower puddles of Luther lore. This idea, however is a "bigly" myth—and a significant issue in Christian history. Did Luther intend to establish an independent church, separate from Catholicism? Did he actually want to begin a "Lutheran" church?

No, this is another myth of the Reformation and a surprising one, perhaps. Who wouldn't want to change the course of history and stamp it with one's own name? Well, Luther for one.

The misunderstanding behind this myth arose from Luther's preface to *The German Mass and Order of Divine Service* (1526) in which he said:

It must be that those who want to be with earnest Christians and profess the gospel with deeds and words, sign up and meet anywhere in a house to pray, read, baptize, receive communion, and do other Christian works. . . . Here one could have a general offering, where one gives freely as well as to the poor, following the example of Saint Paul (2 Cor. 9:1). . . . In short, if one had the people who want to be with earnest Christians, the rules and structures would soon be made. However, I cannot and would not like to direct or set up such a community or gathering quite yet because for this I have no people.[1]

To step back for a moment: one of the reasons independent evangelical churches are independent is because there are people who freely choose to join that church. No one becomes a church member without agreeing to it. This voluntary aspect requires, however, a few things:

1. A rejection of infant baptism (if one assumes this makes the infant a "member")
2. A conscious decision to want to live as a Christian (rather than being a "cultural Christian" on Christmas and Easter)
3. The separation of church and state (so that being born a citizen does not automatically make one a church member)

Some of the more well-known independent evangelical churches that followed the subsequent religious turmoil of the Reformation are the Mennonites, the Baptists, the Evangelical Free Church, and the Brethren Church.[2]

With the exception of the Mennonites, none of these independent churches are older than four hundred years. What all these groups have in common is that they organize their bylaws and structures *congregationally* for the most part. That means that the whole community (and community only) decides on the contents and forms of organization. There is no overarching structure that dictates church policy, a system we now commonly call "denominationalism." The right of the laity to preach, lead church services, and carry out sacramental acts such as communion, baptism, marriages, and funerals is practiced in most independent churches. This "grassroots democracy" in questions of faith leads naturally to an

---

1. Bornkamm and Ebeling, *Martin Luther*, vol. 5, 77.
2. Of course, scores and scores of denominations, sects, and cults have arisen since the Reformation, but most have no direct connection to Luther. Some have no direct connection to Christianity, for that matter.

abundant diversity in doctrines and theological convictions. Which is either horribly extreme or exactly right, depending on one's point of view.

While a Roman Catholic Mass is always the same in every language of the world from rural Montana to Rome, independent church services and forms of piety can vary every fifty miles. One may find that fascinating or confusing, impressive or strange; one may label an independent church-goer as "charismatic" or "evangelical" or both and understand this as a mark of quality or as a warning sign. What they all have in common is that they "want to be with earnest Christians," "read their Bibles in their houses, pray, profess the gospel with their words and deeds, do Christian works" and—very importantly—"give offerings." The strict separation of church and state means, at the bottom line, that the church does not col-lect tax revenue on behalf of the state. Independent churches provide not only all personal, operational, and programmatic costs exclusively from the donations of their members but also all that they "give to the poor," which amounts to millions of dollars annually for health care, social work, education, development, and missions.

Are independent churches then indeed a later development of what Martin Luther could only dream of? For which he unfortunately didn't have "any people"?

No, not at all. From 1518 onward Luther was indeed a wanted man and a searched-after heretic, but in his thinking, feeling, and believ-ing he remained a true Catholic. The Reformation notwithstanding, he remained a thoroughly medieval person, in whose worldview "society" (on the large scale) and "community" (on the small scale) were still one and the same. Because all people were baptized—more on that later— all were Christians to begin with, believers in the one and only church, period. Those "wanting to be with earnest Christians"—these were, in Luther's thought, the especially dedicated Christians. If they met in house groups to pray and others didn't, that was not for Luther a categorical distinction between Christians and non-Christians.

Whoever wanted to be "unbelieving" fell not only from the church but also out of every social community in the medieval world (which has also been the case in very Catholic regions of the world even into the twentieth century).

During Luther's time, the emperor and pope fought over supremacy. There were two systems of justice in the same territory: the "worldly" authority (kings and princes) and the "ecclesiastical" authority (popes and bishops)—and this was problematic enough. The state protected and supported the church, and the church legitimized and authorized the state. Did this holy marriage of kingly throne and popish altar divorce intentionally and say good-bye, creating the independence of the state from the church? In the sixteenth century of Martin Luther, such a bold position was hardly yet conceivable.

But did Luther indeed attack the order of the church and, through that, indirectly shake the order of the state and society?

Precisely. And, to be honest, he became afraid of his own "courage." Large numbers of monks and nuns were deserting their monasteries. Priests quit their ministry. Others stood as newlywed men in front of their congregations. In the Mass, the priest passed not only the host but also the cup. The formerly revered mendicants, or poor monks, were being pelted with stones by students. The pulpit was becoming politically polemicized. The people were anxious. Who actually still ensured legal certainty? The social order seemed to be slipping into anarchy.

Beginning on May 4, 1521, while Luther was stuck in Wartburg castle, his colleague at the university and ally, Andreas Bodenstein von Karlstadt, curtly cancelled the sacrosanct Mass for Christmas 1521 and celebrated a simple "new" communion. In January 1522, Karlstadt, along with Philip Melanchthon, wrote up their own order of worship and allowed holy images to be ripped from the walls and publicly burned. "Rebuke organs, trumpets, and flutes at the theater!"[3] was his battle cry.

Worse was to come from the town of Zwickau. Three cloth weavers— Nicholas Storch, Markus Stübner, and Thomas Drechsel—arrived in Wittenberg and brought with them seventy-two "disciples" who preached

---

3. Birnstein, *Who is Who der Reformation*, 59.

confused sermons riddled with Bible verses about the imminent end of the world and God's judgment over all civil authority. One of these radicals was Thomas Müntzer (see chapter 16, "Luther Was the First Lutheran"), who sympathized with the rebellious farmers who supported the radical preachers.

Luther sensed that he had lit a fuse, which ran straight to a powder keg beneath the princes and the royal courts. Just one spark and all the pillars of the social order would come tumbling down around him. He returned from the Wartburg on March 9, 1522, went right to the pulpit of the state church and . . . stepped on the brakes of this runaway train (metaphorically, of course; the train was still to be invented). "No revolution, people, just small-scale and well-dosed reforms, please"—that was the key message.

The seventh Sunday before Easter is called Invocavit Sunday in the church calendar. Luther held a so-called Invocavit sermon against the radical reformers. He ranted against the "prophets of Zwickau" with some success: Philip Melanchthon, who had joined the radical cause, went back to his friend Luther, repentant. Andreas Bodenstein von Karlstadt bolted off to Orlamünde in southeast Germany in the summer of 1523; there he abolished infant baptism and the confessional and introduced the lay chalice (individual believers partaking of the cup). Thomas Müntzer was deeply disappointed by Martin Luther and labeled him "Father Pussyfoot." The seventy-two disciples in Zwickau, meanwhile, found a sympathetic ear with the rebellious farmers in the hills and forests of central Germany.

It is not really totally fair for state church ministers to reflexively quote Martin Luther's warning against the "radical reformers" when expressing their reluctance about the forms of piety found in independent churches.[4] Luther did not warn against enthusiastic prayer poses or fervent song

---

4. Such ministers would most likely be found in Germany, Denmark, Iceland, Norway, Finland, or Sweden, where the Lutheran church is recognized as the state church or has special status—which admittedly sounds strange to American believers who celebrate the separation of church and state in the US Constitution.

lyrics—he warned against enthusiastic, radical social romanticism, political naivety, and pious anarchy in the state and church. Seriously—none of this is to be feared from the independent churches in the twenty-first century.

Thinking back for a moment: Luther did away with so much—why not infant baptism as well? Branches of the Lutheran church today believe that "when an infant is baptized God creates faith in the heart of that infant."[5] It may seem like a minor issue, but it actually had a major place in Luther's thinking and in his view of the individual, the church, and the state. So why did Luther hang on to infant baptism, something other reformers rejected?

Short answer: because Luther was (despite all his disagreements with the church) a quintessential Catholic in his thoughts and feelings. In his understanding, each person is from the moment of conception burdened with original sin. As descendants of the fallen human couple Adam and Eve, every person needs a "remedy for original sin," as the church father Augustine of Hippo said.[6] Baptism was endowed by God ("principal cause"), administered by a priest ("intentional cause"), and carried out with consecrated water ("instrumental cause")—so it has been defined since 1439 in the papal bull[7] "Exsultate Deo." This was binding for Luther and is, by the way, valid even today in the Catholic Church. Baptism was understood as the visibly received promise from God to forgive the sins of humanity. As a ritual, it portrayed God's covenant with his people, and was a symbol of God's continuing mercy.

Baptism was for Luther the visible integration of people into the earthly body of the risen Christ, and thus into the church. Redemption from original sin and our belonging to the body of the risen Christ therefore justifies the inclusion of humans in the eternal bliss of heaven after death.

Death, however, occurred most frequently during infancy throughout

---

5. "Frequently Asked Questions," The Lutheran Church—Missouri Synod.
6. Augustine of Hippo, "Enchiridion."
7. This is, of course, neither an animal or idle watercooler chatter, but a religious document issued by the pope that gets its name from the lead seal (*bulla*—Latin for "lead") attached as authentication.

Luther's time. When one reads how swiftly and with such ceremonial and strenuous effort newborns were baptized, we can get a sense of the gripping fear parents had that their child could die unbaptized and thereby fall prey to the devil. For a quick look at the thinking of the times, consider Luther's instructions to the priests in his "Baptismal Booklet" from 1526:

> Therefore please remember that it is by no means a light matter or a bit of fun to take sides against the devil and not only to drive him away from the little child but to load on his little shoulders such a mighty and life-long enemy.
>
> Remember, that the external rituals of baptism are the least important. Hence, blowing into the eyes, making the sign of the cross, giving salt in the mouth, putting spittal and clay in the ears and nose, anointing the breast and shoulders with oil, spreading the oil of anointing on the head, putting on the christening robe, placing burning candles in the hand, . . . a baptism can occur without any of these things. The devil surely ridicules even grander things, so therefore there must be a seriousness in everything.
>
> The baptizer shall say:
>
> "Come out, you unclean spirit!" And afterward you make a cross on the forehead and chest of the child. Let us pray: "I summon you, you unclean spirit, in name of the Father and of the Son and of the Holy Spirit, that you come out and vanish from this servant of Jesus Christ, (name of the child), Amen!"
>
> Afterward the priest allows the child through the godparents to refuse the devil and speak: "Do you renounce the devil?" Response of the godparents: "Yes." And all his works? Response of the godparents: "Yes." "Do you want to be baptized?" Response of the godparents: "Yes." Then the priest takes the child and dips the child into the baptism font.[8]

---

8. Müller, *Die symbolischen Bücher der evangelische-lutherischen Kirche*, 835.

Baptism in Luther's understanding from 1526 presupposes the Christian faith. Of course not the individual faith of the child, but of the parents, godparents, and church. One could say that the infant "believes vicariously." Baptism was for the redemption of original sin and necessary for salvation, it is a means of God's grace, it has to a great extent the function of an exorcism (!), and it could not be carried out soon enough due to the high rate of infant mortality. In this, Luther knew himself to be in good company: in the times of the first Christians, many let themselves be baptized immediately, including their entire household—children, slaves, relatives, and wives—(as did the Roman officer Cornelius in Acts 10:48 and the fabric dyer Lydia in Acts 16:15). One of the earliest ecclesiastical orders comes from the year AD 215, when the church father Hippolytus of Rome regulated the "*baptismus infantium*,"[9] the baptism of children (not "infantile Baptists").[10]

"Therefore please remember that it is by no means a light matter or a bit of fun to take sides against the devil."

Of course, others during that time saw things very differently. And how! For example, in Zurich the reformer and Bible translator Ulrich Zwingli held that baptism was a sacrament, but he did not primarily attribute to it the washing away of sins and an exorcism effect. Rather, he saw it as the conclusion to God's covenant with the person baptized that emphasized the resulting belonging to God's people. For Zwingli, baptism is the New Testament equivalent to Old Testament circumcision.

From January 1519 onward, Zwingli was the priest at the Grossmünster church in Zurich and reformed his Catholic congregation just as radically

---

9. Altaner, *Theologische Real-Enzyklopädie*, 667.
10. A little pun for the Latin enthusiast. Baptism for infants (*baptismus infantium*) versus infantile (*infantilen*) baptism, that is, childish, immature, or silly. For readers who find Latin puns tedious at best, my apologies.

as Luther had done in Wittenberg, only not with as much chaos. Dissolving monasteries, changing the liturgy of the Mass, rewriting the ordinances, redefining the contents—all of it went down a little more quietly in Switzerland. Zwingli's friends and pals from college days were Felix Manz, the illegitimate son of a chaplain, and Conrad Grebel, whose father was a councilman in Zurich (and later would be unjustly executed). The two had one thing in common—a critical relationship to the church and the state. They also had a burning love for Holy Scripture, in which they read that Jesus sent out his disciples to teach people in faith, preach the gospel, and baptize them (Matt. 28:19). They read that Peter cried out while preaching at the first Pentecost, "Repent and be baptized" (Acts 2:38), that Philip "baptized both men and women" (Acts 8:12), and that Paul interpreted baptism as a "burial" of the old person and a "resurrection" of the new person (Rom. 6:3–4).

Felix Manz and Conrad Grebel translated Scripture with this understanding: *first* comes faith and confession, *then* comes baptism. First the conception, then the birth. Not the other way around. "Whoever believes and is [then] baptized will be saved"—they read Jesus's Great Commission in Mark 16:16. And from then on they rejected infant baptism.

Ulrich Zwingli didn't see it the same way as his old college buddies. (People grow apart and friendships cool, I guess!) So the two wrote letters to Thomas Müntzer but were repelled by his radicalness and readiness to use violence. Felix Manz met with Andreas Bodenstein von Karlstadt in Basel, but instead of becoming friends with Wittenberg's "radical reformer," Manz ended up forming a friendship with the Swabian reformer Wilhelm Reublin, who hadn't been baptizing infants for many years at churches in Basel and in the Swiss town of Witikon.[11]

Finally, a showdown between the various parties took place on January 17, 1525: Conrad Grebel, Felix Manz, Wilhelm Reublin, Michael Sattler (formerly head of a Benedictine monastery in the Black Forest), and many other baptism opponents were invited to a "baptism disputation" in front of the city council. There, Ulrich Zwingli prevailed as the proponent of

---

11. Which unfortunately sounds like a town full of smart alecks.

infant baptism. The city council concluded: whoever doesn't let their children be baptized within eight days will be banished from Zurich! So there!

On the evening of January 21, 1525, the losers gathered in the house of Felix Manz's mother. A monk from the monastery of St. Lucius in Grisons, who at the council wore a blue coat and had spoken against infant baptism, was also there: Georg Cajacob (who was nicknamed George "Blaurock" because of his blue coat. Yes, guys teased each other about their clothes even five hundred years ago).

Blaurock stood up and . . . asked Conrad Grebel to baptize him! Everyone was dumbfounded. The air grew electric with anticipation. And . . . Grebel did it. Afterward George Blaurock baptized all the others. Thus the idea of the "Baptists" was formed. This is the original date of the movement, which, as the so-called left wing of the Reformation, has spread up into the twenty-first century with the Dutch Mennonites, the Bohemian Brethren, the Canadian Hutterites, the Eberhard Arnold Bruderhof communities, and the Amish communities in the United States.

So we can ask: Wasn't what was done in the Zurich apartment of Mama Manz just the thing Luther suggested in his preface to *The German Mass*?

One could say so. But the Reformers themselves and the "authorities by God's grace" of the civil government stifled (or worse) many of the radical reformers. Felix Manz, almost thirty years of age, with hands and feet shackled, was thrown into the Limmat River in 1527. (Death by drowning was considered an especially despicable way to die and was usually reserved for adulteresses. Here it was just a cruel joke on being baptized again.) George Blaurock was first tortured on September 6, 1529, in Klausen, in what is now northern Italy, then burned to death. Michael Sattler suffered terribly, having his tongue ripped out in Rottenburg[12] on May 21, 1527, his appendages pinched off with burning forceps, and his torso and head burned at the stake. His wife was drowned in the Neckar

---

12. An appropriate name (*Rotten* means "rotten" in English as well) for the morally rotten actions taken against these innocent victims. (And, irony of history, today Rottenburg is the seat of Germany's southwestern Catholic bishop Gebhard Fürst, a friend of mine since doing some good television interviews.)

River. Only Conrad Grebel died "peacefully" in March 1526 due to the plague, which infected him in prison.

And Luther?

He still understood the rejection of infant baptism as the beginning of a revolutionary, anarchic social upheaval, namely due to his experiences with Andreas Bodenstein and Thomas Müntzer. He gave them the derogative name "*anabaptista*" or "Anabaptists." Because if one baptizes adults due to their *conversion* and their *confession*, then one revokes the already performed infant baptism (the Greek prefix *ana* means "again"). Therefore, these people committed a sacrilege to a sacrament, a means of God's grace. Which to many Christian thinkers, Luther included, was to commit one of the worst blasphemies imaginable. What was unimaginable in the sixteenth century was that parents wouldn't let their infants be baptized or that they would let a child be rebaptized. Unthinkable.

In 1530, Emperor Charles V once again called an imperial diet. This time in Augsburg. The Diet of Worms[13] in 1521 was a political flop, which led only to the Protestation at Speyer in 1529 and divided the particular principalities of Germany into "Lutherans" and "Roman Catholics." Now, as a result, everything had to be done all over again thoroughly from the beginning.

Philip Melanchthon wrote twenty-eight articles to defend the Reformation at the imperial diet and divided them into "common articles" 1–21 (which were united fully with the present Catholic teachings and practices) and "disputed articles" 22–28 (which were to be understood as discussable suggestions for reform). Luther checked the text, gave a nod of assent, and the holiest writing (after the Bible) of the evangelical Lutherans to this day was finished: the *Confessio Augustana*, the "CA," or, most popularly, the Augsburg Confession. It is gladly seen as the "founding document of the evangelical church" by Luther's subsequent followers, which was the complete *opposite* intention of its composers! Even in 1530, Luther wanted to reform the Catholic Church, not split it. Article 9 of

---

13. See chapter 9, "Luther Sometimes Played Tricks and Told Lies," and chapter 12, "Luther Said, 'Here I Stand. I Cannot Do Otherwise.'"

the CA reads, "It is being taught that baptism is necessary; that one is supposed to baptize children, who God delivers through the baptism and who are delivered into his grace. May the Anabaptists be condemned, and those who reject infant baptism and claim that children can be saved without baptism."[14]

And today?

Today sensible Christians on both sides of the baptism issue are trying to avoid the polemical and derogatory terms from that era such as "Wiedertäufer!" (baptism repeaters!) or "Zwangsbeglücker!" (forced-into-heaven Christian!) and make more precise distinctions in their choice of words.[15] Even the words "adult baptism" are in principle not accurate. For members of most evangelical churches, it's not about being an adult ("When is one an adult?" one may legitimately ask) but rather it is about the voluntary decision and profession of the individual. "Believers' baptism" is a more accurate term.[16]

If a ten-year-old confesses his or her faith in a free church and wants to be baptized, then they will be. "Infant baptism?" Not really. Theologically, this is very distinct from the nursing baby in arms in the state church.

The evangelical Methodist Church, which arose in England in the eighteenth century, baptized both children and adults. The free evangelical churches, which arose in Germany in the nineteenth century, baptized only people who made a confession of faith, and they also accepted as members those who didn't want to be baptized *again*. The Baptists and Brethren churches, which arose in the United States and England in the nineteenth century, left the decision to their local congregations: some required each person who wanted to become a member to be baptized without fuss or quibble. They didn't perceive this as being baptized *again* because the previous infant baptism was for them null and void. More

---

14. Bornkamm, *Das Augsburger Bekenntnis*, 20.

15. You have to hand it to those Christians in the sixteenth century—they really could sling the insults.

16. To be even more precise, we could say "credobaptism," from the Latin word *credo*, meaning "I believe." Such is the standard of baptism for most Baptist, Mennonite, Pentecostal, and Church of Christ denominations.

and more congregations, however, also accepted members without a person being baptized *again*, if they retrospectively recognized their infant baptism in their confession of faith (and perhaps didn't subsequently want to place the faith of their parents and godparents in the realm of heresy).

Even the Mennonites—historically the "real" baptizers back then—and the Lutheran state church passed in 1996 a "Common Explanation to the Eucharistic Preparedness of Guests" (translation: intercommunion between the two groups). Not to be outdone, the Baptists and the Lutheran state church in Bavaria in 2009 agreed upon a "fundamental consensus in the gospel structuring of baptism and communion."

Would Martin Luther today, five hundred years later, rewrite his preface to *The German Mass* and say, "Finally, I would have the people to establish such a congregation"? An interesting question to ponder.

Chapter 9

Luther Sometimes Played Tricks and Told Lies

Yes, he played at least two tricks and lied once (that we can tell). That's no myth.

On August 7, 1518, Luther received a summons to Rome to be questioned as a heretic (a one-way ticket to be burned at the stake, that much was clear). Luther was friends with George Spalatin, the secretary of Frederick the Wise, prince of Saxony. The Saxon prince had political ambitions to expand the influence of his domain—he was the pope's favorite to succeed the Holy Roman Emperor Maximilian I—but Frederick (remember, he's wise) decided to throw his support behind Maximilian's choice, his grandson Charles, while at the same time extracting from Charles a limit on the emperor's power. Score one point for Frederick. At the same time Cardinal Thomas Cajetan, by order of the pope, wanted to implement an additional tax for a crusade against the Turks (yes, this gets a little complicated!).

Luther wrote to his friend George Spalatin on August 8, saying, "You should appear in person in front of the princes and find out to what extent our prince and his imperial highness could work with the pope so that my case will be passed on to *trial in Germany*."[1]

---

1. Mayer, *Martin Luther*, 72.

Pretty bold, huh? A poor monk in trouble asks the secretary of state to ask the prince to ask the emperor to ask the pope for something for Luther! Frederick of Saxony knew that Cardinal Cajetan still wanted something from him (mainly money for a war), and so he got Luther's summons to Rome changed to Augsburg (score two for Frederick and one for Luther; pope zero).

Luther made his appearance at the diet, defended his theses from October 12 to 14 in the Augsburg city palace in Augsburg in front of the cardinal, and in doing so uttered the fatal line, "Even the pope doesn't stand over, but rather under, the Word of God!" With these words, Luther was being seasoned for the grill. Thomas Cajetan, however, did nothing. He pushed back the date for another hearing, giving Luther a chance to apologize, and remained silent.

> "Even the pope doesn't stand over,
> but rather under, the Word of God!"

It became still in Augsburg. Disturbingly still. A war of nerves. Luther allowed a letter of protest to be delivered to the representative of the pope stating that he wanted to continue to talk—but then escaped secretly in the night from the city on October 21. He stalled his enemies in order to skedaddle—that's certainly playing a trick!

Three years later, once again at a diet in the city of Worms, a similar scene played out. On April 25, 1521, the young Emperor Charles V arranged for the rhetorically skillful and stubborn-about-the-text Luther to be given imperial protection for twenty-one days, long enough for the return trip to Wittenberg. Was it short-term life insurance or a trap? *"A fuego, a fuego!"* Charles's Spanish knights whispered as Luther passed by them. "Into the fire, into the fire!"

Luther left Worms on May 3 and the day after was "held up" by "bandits" on the road and "kidnapped." Luther was spirited away to the Wartburg castle in Eisenach (his mother's hometown, safely in Saxony) and tucked away under the name "Sir George." Frederick the Wise and his faithful secretary, George Spalatin, Luther's friend, organized the whole thing (this is still being discussed somewhat by historians). That Luther was in the know about his capture may be postulated. Luther had earlier written to the painter Lucas Cranach, "I'll let myself be done in and hidden. I myself still don't know where. It must be kept silent and waited out."[2]

But—who put out the rumor that Luther was discovered in a silver mine in the Thuringian Forest? Dead, of course, pierced by a sword? The rumor spread so quickly that the Nuremberg painter Albrecht Dürer, while in faraway Holland at the time, wrote in his diary, "Does he still live or have they killed him? Oh God, is Luther dead—who will henceforth bring forward the holy gospel so clearly?"[3]

Only at the ongoing Diet of Worms, one individual had strong doubts about this oh-so-convenient homicide: Emperor Charles V.

On May 26, he set forth an imperial ban, a condemnation of Luther and a revocation of all rights, named the Edict of Worms. Through this, the emperor confirmed the bull of excommunication issued by the pope, but now intensified it as a state proclamation, giving each and every loyal citizen the right to carry out vigilante justice: "being demanded that no one provide Luther with shelter, food, drink, nor provide help, secretly or publicly, support, or further transportation. Instead, wherever you come upon him, use force to take him captive and send him to us safe and sound."[4]

"Send him to us safe and sound," mind you. They wanted to do the torture part themselves. Such cynicism burns the tongue.

Did the prince of Saxony know that his protégé had long since been in safety? At the imperial diet, Frederick the Wise acted as Frederick the Clueless.

Emperor Charles V played, however, a trick of his own: he dated the

2. Süßenguth, *Aus einem traurigen Arsch*, 47.
3. Ibid., 50.
4. Ibid.

imperial ban *back* to May 8, 1521! With this date, it looked as if this so-called Edict of Worms had been decided upon by *everyone* at the imperial diet. (If you are still keeping score, one point for Charles.) However, the various princes who had already left couldn't remember having discussed or approved any such thing on May 8, so they refused to play a part in the Luther chase over the following eight years. The eventual split-up of Germany into Lutheran and Catholic principalities and cities was thus under way.

Whatever the emperor could do, so could "Sir George" as well: Luther wrote a letter to George Spalatin on July 15, 1521:

> Greetings in Christ, dear Mr. Spalatin. As I hear, one is spreading the rumor that Luther is dwelling in the Wartburg castle in Eisenach. Because I was captured there in the woods, the people are coming to this assumption. In the unlikely event that I'm betrayed by the announcement of my writings, I will change my whereabouts. It's a good thing that no one will think of Bohemia.[5]

Sorry, come again? Bohemia? Enclosed with the letter was an accompanying explanation:

> Dear Mr. Spalatin, I have composed the following lie: the rumors of my whereabouts are growing. Even when the people don't dare to claim it, one can't be so easily dissuaded from it. Therefore, I'm asking you to *intentionally lose my enclosed letter* or to allow one of your people to allow this carelessness to be committed. That way it should land in the hands of our enemies, who will believe to have wrongfully gotten possession of a strictly confidential secret. It would be most wonderful if it fell into hands of the pig from Dresden [George, Duke of Saxony, an enemy of the Reformation]. He would joyfully make known at once its

---

5. Dithmar, *Durch Gottes Gnade bin ich wohlauf,* 36.

contents. Do that which seems advisable. I hope for improvement. Farewell in Christ. From solitude, 1521, yours, Dr. Martinus.[6]

The trick with the false trail worked, it seems. Luther would remain until March 1, 1522, unbetrayed in the Wartburg castle as he translated the New Testament into German. So another point for Luther, with the final score being Frederick three, Luther two, and Charles (the loser) one.

Of course, Luther's ruse with the letter wasn't true, and therefore a lie, in the technical sense of the word. In Colossians 3:9 we read the admonition: "Do not lie to each other." Perhaps Luther had not gotten around to translating that Scripture yet.

---

6. Ibid., 35.

Chapter 10

Luther Married in Secret

This Luther myth is neither fish nor fowl but only halfway true. On June 27, 1525, Katharina von Bora and Martin Luther were married publicly and fully unsecretly in the city church of Wittenberg. But two weeks before, there had been a private wedding in Luther's apartment on June 13, 1525.

Present was Father Johannes Bugenhagen, friends Justus Jonas and the married couple Barbara and Lucas Cranach, and the lawyer Johann Apel. With five witnesses from public life in Wittenberg, it wasn't sooo terribly secret but nevertheless, yes, granted, it was done on the sly. Luther would later comment, "If I hadn't consummated the marriage in full secrecy, everyone would have deterred me from it. 'Just not her, but another,' so my best friends would have advised."[1]

Martin put a golden ring on his Katharina's finger, accompanied by a cone-shaped box. The ring could be split apart and contained a small ruby and the engraving "MLD and CVB, therefore what God has joined together, let no one separate."[2]

Was it love at first sight? Huh, no. Six of the nine nuns who escaped to Wittenberg during the turmoil of the Reformation were successfully

---

1. Mayer, *Martin Luther*, 136.
2. Süßenguth, *Aus einem traurigen Arsch*, 84.

brought to safety or returned to their families of origin. Two couldn't return home because that would have placed them in the domain of George, Duke of Saxony, who did not tolerate "Lutheran heretics" nor runaway nuns. One of the two nuns, however, did not want to go to either her stepparents or Pastor Kaspar Glatz, whom Luther had located for her. That nun was Katharina von Bora.

"God wanted it that I have pity on the remaining nun," recalled Luther later, "although at the beginning, I held Katharina to be suspicious, proud, and haughty. But I fared well with her. I've gotten a faithful and dependable woman."[3]

Did Katharina have good cause to feel like a piece of furniture from a garage sale? In our way of thinking about romance today—yes. But a romantic love marriage in which an individual actually *chose* a partner was the rare exception in 1525. An arranged marriage above all—if it materialized consensually—was certainly better than a *forced* marriage.

That Luther married the ex-nun "in order that I, with confidence in offspring, finally no longer oppose my father's last wish" (mining entrepreneur Hans Luther still wanted to see a grandchild before he died) was for Katharina, in the thinking of her time, fully legitimate and not just a lousy reason.[4]

How did Luther's friends react? Surprised. But in different ways.

George Spalatin at the court of Prince Frederick the Wise sent one hundred gulden as a wedding present.[5] Nicolaus von Amsdorf and escape-helper Leonhard Köppe promised to come to the "official" wedding celebration on June 27, 1525. But Luther's co-translator of the Bible, personal friend and intellectual Philip Melanchthon, was appalled. To be on the safe side Melanchthon wrote in Greek to an acquaintance in Nuremberg: "He is of course the easiest man to manipulate, and the nuns, who understand these tricks, have brought him so far. All of the contact with them has made him soft; to be sure it has also ignited itself in his nature,

---

3. Mayer, *Martin Luther*, 136.
4. Ibid.
5. A rather generous gift of between $6,000 and $10,000 in today's currency.

and therefore he seems to have fallen into the old-fashioned change of life."[6] Luther's "nature has ignited itself"? Uh-huh. In plain language: Melanchthon believed that twenty-six-year-old Katharina had seduced the forty-two-year-old professor.

So what exactly *did* former celibate monk Martin Luther think about sex?

> "So many awful things confront me daily in the miserable celibacy of the young men and women that nothing is more despicable to my ears than the titles nun, monk, and priest."

For his time, Luther's attitude was incredibly humane and favorable. None of the words *sexuality, sex,* or *eroticism* even existed yet, and of "intercourse" absolutely nothing is said. But behind the awkward-sounding terms of his time, one reads clearly how glowingly he valued sex and marriage, even if the picture is less than transparent. As a responsible district vicar and father confessor of the monks at eleven monasteries, Luther was familiar with everything humane as well as inhumane. Which is why he developed a downright hatred of mandatory celibacy: "So many awful things confront me daily in the miserable celibacy of the young men and women that nothing is more despicable to my ears than the titles nun, monk, and priest."[7] Or: "The nefarious and harmful superstition of celibacy and the unmarried lives of the clerics in the papacy has caused abominable sins and promoted the same: prostitution, adultery, incest, wetness, indecent dreams, strange apparitions and faces during sleep as well as ejaculations and impurities."[8] This presumably means: ecclesiastical men acted out their sexual fantasies with prostitutes, married women, female relatives, and possibly also with children. And even to delusional images.

---

6. Schmidt-König, *Käthe Luther*, 20.
7. Diwald, *Luther*, 246.
8. Krumbholz, *Euch stoßen*, 108.

However, Luther distinguished sharply between the abuse of sexuality and the God-created gift itself: "It is a necessary, natural thing that a man has a wife and a wife a man. When one wants to deny that, which is not to be opposed, he goes on his way through prostitution, adultery, and stupid sins."[9]

In short: Luther held that the sexual urge of humanity is irresistible and that this irresistibility was not a mistake by the creator but rather pointed to the ethical task of people. Luther knew that neither (the celibate) Jesus nor (the unmarried) Paul made singleness a requirement for the clergy. He knew that celibacy was not even canonically a dogma, but rather only a decree of the church. Only Roman Catholic priests had to remain celibate while Orthodox priests in eastern and southern Europe were allowed to marry. Luther knew that celibacy had been contested for almost one thousand years, and it hadn't become obligatory until 1139. Not that the asexual life seemed to him to be an excessive demand—but the pledge itself misses the reality of people: "Yes, we have promised and vowed to God that we want to be chaste and live without women. To this I say: that is downright tomfoolery. Why do you promise to do that when you don't know whether you are able to keep it? I have made one promise to myself, which I can also keep: never to cut off my own nose!"[10]

And the women?

"Now take a look at the sorrow of the other part: there are, to a large extent, girls in monasteries who are fresh and healthy and created by God so that they become women and shall carry children. A girl who is not able to remain single out of conviction can no more deny herself and go without a man as she can go without food, drink, sleep, or any other natural need. In turn, a man cannot deny himself a woman. Wherever reluctant abstinence is, human nature doesn't stop acting. That I crudely state: flow it not in the flesh, so flow it in the shirt!"[11]

---

9. Zitelmann, *Ich, Martin Luther*, 16.
10. Schilling, *Luther zum Vergnügen*, 69.
11. Zitelmann, *Ich, Martin Luther*, 14.

And even when a man allows a surgical end to the "work of nature"[12]—as was done to the harem guards in the Ottoman Empire or the castrated sopranos in Europe's opera houses—the "work of nature" remained working in the head and heart. "Eunuchs burn more than all others," Luther said in bewilderment. "Then with the snip, it is not the desire that leaves, but rather only the ability. I wanted rather to leave my pair attached than having them cut off!"[13]

Let me say that it is wonderful that we can talk so freely about these subjects (if you're still reading, that is).

But the cherished and willed-by-God naturalness of sexuality nonetheless did not work as an excuse for Luther. The practice of having mistresses for example (which was common practice for the priests, monks, and nobles of Luther's time) didn't cut it: "Celibacy means not loving women but rather loving the mortification and shame of women. Furthermore, it means not treating them as women but rather as prostitutes so that henceforth no one may have love nor respect for them."[14] To have "love and respect"? The phrase "human dignity" didn't exist at the time, but Luther's standard of appreciation and respect for women is unmistakable.

By the way, he was also of the opinion that one is not supposed to separate sex and love and that both come together ideally in marriage: "This is the reason and the entire essence of marriage that one gives one's self to the other and finds his or her delight in the other, but the spirit, heart, and gender must ring together."[15] And: "The greatest grace of God is when love in marriage blooms enduringly. The first love is fiery, an inebriated love. When we've slept off the intoxication, then remains in piety the real marital love. But for the godless remains remorse."[16]

Then what was it like for Mr. and Mrs. Luther? Did their marital love blossom?

---

12. And not so surgically—emasculation could take several brutal forms.
13. Henkys, *Luthers Tischreden*, 149.
14. Zitelmann, *Ich, Martin Luther*, 21.
15. Winter, *Katharina von Bora*, 134.
16. Aland, *Luther deutsch*, 274.

And how! A well-known Luther quote honestly reveals Luther's initial anxiety: "In the first year of marriage one has odd thoughts. In bed, you see a pair of pigtails next to yourself, which you had never seen before."[17] Or: "I often laid with my Kathy, and although she is a lovable woman, I would break out in a cold sweat."[18] But that he, the former monk, over time learned an erotic tenderness is revealed in a candid quote that is surprising (and for that time considered scandalous): "With the woman, with whom God has joined me, joking, playing, and talking affectionately are allowed."[19]

When one reads all the letters that Luther wrote his Katharina—and introduced with euphorically devised attestations of honor such as "Doctor," "Lady," "Gardner,"—the picture of a great romantic love untypical for the time emerges, which grew with each year of their twenty-one-year marriage: "Not for the sake of France or Venice would I have wanted to part from my Kathy. She was given to me by God, as I also was to her. She is a faithful woman and her virtues are much greater than her shortcomings."[20]

Would the Luthers—as a Catholic couple in their own estimation—have practiced contraception? If so, it didn't always work out: Katharina Luther brought their first son, Johannes, into the world on June 7, 1526, one year after the wedding and breastfed him for ten months. As she nevertheless already became pregnant with a second child, Martin Luther was surprised and said, "It is hard to feed two guests: the one in the house and the other at the front door."[21]

As far as the topic of birth control goes, there's nothing more to be found. The couple had six kids in nine years. Johannes, Elizabeth (died at nine months), Magdalena (died at thirteen years old), Martin Jr., Paul, and Margarete.

And did the reformer do his turn at the diaper-changing table? Most

---

17. Fausel, *D. Martin Luther*, 92.
18. Zitelmann, *Ich, Martin Luther*, 21.
19. Brecht, *Martin Luther: Die Erhaltung der Kirche*, 235.
20. Schmidt-König, *Käthe Luther*, 37.
21. Saager, *Luther-Anekdoten*, 187.

probably. He defended himself for doing it at least once and justified baby
care by the father even theologically:

> If a man goes and washes the diapers or does any other disdain-
> ful work for a child, and everyone mocks him and holds him
> for a monkey's mouth or woman's man, although he is doing it
> indeed in Christian faith. . . . God smiles with all the angels and
> creatures! Not that he washes the diapers, but rather that he does
> so in Christian faith. Those who sneer at him, who only see the
> work and don't want to see the faith, mock God with all his crea-
> tures as the biggest fool on earth. They mock only themselves and
> are monkey mouths of the devil for all their cleverness![22]

One is tempted to describe the relationship of the couple as a modern
marriage!

The two-week "secret" Luther marriage only lasted between June 13
and June 27, 1525, but for one of Luther's prominent followers, his unsanc-
tioned "marriage" stretched on for years. On August 4, 1545, half a year
before his death, Martin Luther greeted the cathedral dean Sigismund
von Lindenau in the Merseburg Cathedral and his "wife" at the altar.

The two had already been "married" seven years without the church's
sanction. Luther was there to see that Sigismund finally made her an "honest woman," as we say.

---

22. Schorlemmer, *Hier stehe ich,* 136.

Chapter 11

Luther's Wife Traveled to Him in a Fish Barrel

No, she traveled in a horse carriage, which had barrels of herring tucked away under a cover. She also didn't go to him, rather first to . . . well, let's start from the beginning.

Katharina von Bora, born on January 29, 1499, was the fourth child of a noble family from Lippendorf near Leipzig. Her mother died early. The withdrawn stepmother didn't like the little girl. Katharina was shipped off to the Marienthron Monastery at the fragile age of six. Why there? The abbess (boss) of the monastery was a distant relative on her mother's side, Margarete von Haubitz.

Whoever didn't hear the explosive directives of this howitzer[1] of an abbess was severely disciplined. But Kathy was a bright child and the 367 relics of the monastery gave her comfort: a splinter from Jesus's manger in Bethlehem, a splinter from the communion table from the upper room, chips from his cross on Calvary and from the cross of the condemned next to him. (How convenient that one could distinguish all these types of wood.)

On October 15, 1515, during a celebratory service, Katharina made her

---

1. A howitzer (artillery gun) in German is *haubitze*. A little pun on the abbess's name Haubitz.

vows and at the age of sixteen became a nun of the Cistercian order.[2] At that time, there was also a monastery of Augustinian monks in close proximity, whose abbot, Wolfgang von Zeschau, enjoyed reading the newest books written by an Augustinian colleague from Wittenberg. *Concerning the Monk's Vow*, for example, or *On the Freedom of a Christian*. In these works one reads: "A woman was not made to remain a virgin, but rather to bear children. How many 'happy and delighted nuns,' do you think, are in the cloisters, who are not forced to perform the office and carry the order? In a thousand, hardly one!"[3]

"My young nieces should also read that," Wolfgang thought—and sent over Luther's writings to the nuns' cloister. To Margarete and Veronika von Zeschau and their friend, Katharina von Bora. The girls were inspired. In youthful boisterousness, they asked their families that they be allowed to return to normal life. How did Kathy's stepmother react to that? Almost the same as when she shipped the cheeky little miss off to the monastery! "Stay where you are" was the harsh response. After that Katharina started to think about her escape.

Every other Saturday, a horse carriage rumbled into the courtyard of the Marienthron Monastery. The company supplying household goods and groceries run by Leonhard Köppe was there once again. Today we would say that a pizza and Amazon delivery arrived at the door at the same time. The servants of the sixty-year-old councilman Köppe unloaded iron tools and small parts, but first and foremost the barrels of herring, dried cod, and beer. The wagon brought full barrels and took back the empty ones (medieval recycling, as it were). Such was the case on the evening of April 4, the Easter Saturday of 1523. Oddly enough, on that day the boss was personally sitting in the carriage. And loading up all the empty containers took so long.

Not until early on Sunday morning—an Easter morning to boot—did

---

2. A "reform" by her time that was almost five hundred years old and stressed strict obedience to the rule of St. Benedict and self-reliance through manual labor in farming and food production.
3. Winter, *Katharina von Bora*, 25–26.

the gunnery sergeant Haubitz realize that twelve nuns were missing. Twelve! And in keeping with the thinking of her time, she didn't immediately suspect Leonhard Köppe, but rather believed "the devil himself took the brides of Christ."[4] Naturally.

Who orchestrated it? The experts are still discussing it. A letter written jointly by the twelve eager-to-flee nuns was given to Martin Luther, and he was supposedly the guilty party. This version was told by Luther's admirers and later also Luther himself. (So to some extent Luther was the reason that nuns would abandon monasteries.) A much different version was circulated intentionally by Luther's despisers: it was an abduction for the trafficking of the girls. In this scenario, Luther would have been issued the death penalty (according to the laws of the kingdom, mind you!). In the Saxon town of Mittweida, a liberator of nuns had been recently beheaded. Perhaps, in this way, a fuse was being lit that would lead inevitably to Luther.

However historically probable this may be, there is a much more probable but unspectacular version: Luther did indeed receive a "begging letter" from the nuns, but meanwhile, the abbot Wolfgang von Zeschau had already asked the dry-goods merchant to liberate his nieces.

Twenty-four hours after their escape, the ladies sat in Torgau in the first evangelical church service of their lives. "*German* Mass," they said, because before that the holy celebration of Mass had always been in Latin. Three women stayed on there with their relatives. On the Tuesday after Easter, the nine others traveled some sixty miles farther to Wittenberg: Elsa von Canitz, Magdalene Staupitz, Ave Grossin, the sisters Margarete and Ave von Schönfeld, Lameta von Gohlis, the sisters Katharina and Margarete von Zeschau (the nieces of the abbot)—and Katharina von Bora. Seven of the nine were daughters of noblemen.

Behind the city church, the Wittenberg jurist and magistrate Philip Reichenbach had a large house where all nine nuns first found accommodation. The confined space didn't last long: some moved on to reunite with relatives, Margarete von Schönfeld married her abductor (!), and

---

4. Wolf, *Luther*, 223.

Katharina von Bora lived and worked shortly thereafter with the Cranach family. The father, Lucas, was a famous painter, and the mother, Barbara, ran a pharmacy. Little Lucas Jr. was eight years old and also wanted to become a painter.

Luther's discreet suggestion to his students that the choices in the marriage market were pleasantly increasing in the two-thousand-person backwater town of Wittenberg was quickly understood by a theology student from a rich home: Jerome Baumgärtner. He was "courting" Katharina (in plain English: flirting like crazy)—and she fell in love with him. The two wanted to marry, but Baumgärtner's parents in faraway Nuremberg refused steadfastly. Kathy, the ex-nun? Not a chance! Jerome dropped out of school and left Wittenberg heartbroken. Only his professor didn't give up hope and wrote to the poor boy on October 12, 1524: "By the way, if you want to keep your Kathy von Bora, you'd best hurry up with the deed before she is given to another who is nearby at hand. She hasn't yet overcome her love for you. I would certainly be happy if you both would be joined together."[5]

> "If you want to keep your Kathy von Bora, you'd best hurry up with the deed before she is given to another. . . . I would certainly be happy if you both would be joined together."

This letter brings at least two questions to mind: How does a forty-two-year-old bachelor professor come to know that the heart of a twenty-five-year-old maiden has "not yet overcome" a broken love?

Answer: Luther knew it from Katharina's housemother, Barbara Cranach, and her painting husband, Lucas. He was friends with the family.

Second, who is the "another who is nearby at hand"?

Answer: His name was Kaspar Glatz. He was once rector of the University of Wittenberg and was then a pastor in Orlamünde, a small town

---

5. Aland, *Die Werke Martin Luthers*, 146.

in Thuringia. Luther wanted to set the two of them up—but Katharina refused! She sent the suitor packing.

The good Father Glatz was hurt,[6] Luther was cross, and the young Ms. von Bora was baffled. She didn't have the guts to speak with the famous reformer in person and therefore asked to speak with Nicolaus von Amsdorf, the philosophy lecturer and a friend of Luther's. She reported to him that Kaspar Glatz was dishonest, quarrelsome, and bossy (good intuition—twelve years later, Glatz was suspended from ministry). Amsdorf asked whether she then ever wanted to marry at all. The prospective sweetheart opened her big mouth and said, "I would indeed take you or the doctor, but never Mr. Glatz!"[7]

And with that, the truth was out. Nicolaus von Amsdorf was more flabbergasted than amused. Neither he nor Katharina could have ever imagined that the new religious and political time would also yield such new societal behavior patterns. She was no longer simply to be married, but she was "required" to take whatever man another man found for her? No. A *woman* said who she wanted to marry. She now chose herself. When Amsfeld told Luther that, Luther's first reaction was typically old-school. He clattered about: "She is proud and arrogant! Does she want to then forever mourn the guy from Nuremberg?"

And then the defamation mill started turning again. Catholic pamphleteers heard that one of the liberated nuns had the hots for the sixteen-years-older reformer. Now they finally knew what the real reason for the whole Reformation was: Luther, the "nun stud," the "libertine of concupiscence," just wanted the cloister ladies.[8]

The news of Martin being sought after also reached distant female pen pals. In nearby Franconia there was, for example, the reformer Argula von Grumbach. She turned all negative headlines into positive ones and was happy Luther's wedding plans were coming together. At least that's what she told others. Luther didn't find that funny at all and

---

6. He evidently got over it, as he later married and had children.
7. Schmidt-König, *Käthe Luther*, 17.
8. Wolf, *Thesen*, 82.

wrote on November 30, 1524, to his friend George Spalatin: "That Argula von Grumbach writes to me of wedding plans, I thank you and wonder to myself that such things about me are being gossiped about because much else is also being chatted about. Thank her in my name and tell her: with the attitude which I have, *it will not happen, that I marry*. Not that I wouldn't experience my flesh and gender—I am neither wood nor stone—but my purpose is distant from marriage. Because I daily await death and the rightful punishment for a heretic."[9]

A pious middle-aged man admits to his sexual desires but wants to do without marriage because he is being persecuted? That is exactly the reason the apostle Paul gave during the persecutions of the first century when advising on celibacy (1 Cor. 7:7–9).

And, surprise! A good half year later Luther *was* married. To Katharina. That she still slightly smelled of herring is a myth: Leonhard Köppe didn't put a single escapee in a barrel on April 4, 1523, but merely "brought them out in a covered wagon, as if he was leading out empty herring barrels,"[10] according to a chronicle in Torgau.

But the myth of Kathy in a barrel could also have originated from a tip Luther gave a young man in search of a wife: instead of looking at the income or status of the bride's father, he should look to the character and reputation of the bride's mother. "If one wants to marry, one shouldn't ask about the father, but instead the reputation of the mother because, generally speaking, the beer smells like the barrel from which it came."[11]

Did Luther ever regret the criminal act of aiding an escape? Never. "If God wanted, I would in the same way redeem all captive consciences and make all monasteries empty. I didn't want afterward to shy away in any way from confessing it."[12]

---

9. Birnstein, *Argula von Grumbach*, 67; Wolf, *Thesen*, 160.
10. Piltz, *Daher bin ich*, 118.
11. Aland, *Martin Luther*, 286.
12. Winter, *Katharina von Bora*, 29.

Chapter 12

Luther Said, "Here I Stand.
I Cannot Do Otherwise."

The often forgotten postscript to Luther's famous statement—"God help me, amen"—was officially recorded. "Here I stand. I cannot do otherwise" was not. At the same time, everything that was recorded at the Diet of Worms was not only what Luther said but also what he insinuated. The statement is probably also an admiring but legendary fabrication. Another Luther myth.

What did he actually say then?

During Luther's life, the imperial diet took place once every couple of years and only as needed, a conference summoned at changing locations. *Who* met there was certainly not elected by the people, but they were by all means "representative": the princes, dukes, and counts of the regional principalities, of the "countries," that is. Plus the city representatives who weren't under their respective heads of state, but rather cities that were "free" or "unmediated" by the realm. Plus a pair or two of diplomats from the neighboring kingdoms. Today it would be like a meeting of state leaders, in which the governor, legislators, and mayors of the bigger cities participated. The free city of Worms on the Rhine River had an estimated seven thousand inhabitants in 1521. Among those who were traveling to the diet that year included "eighty princes, 130 counts,

fifteen ambassadors of the lords from foreign countries, many citizens
from imperial cities, and a myriad of people from knights, aristocrats,
and horsemen."[1] Not to mention the beggars, street artists, traders, and
prostitutes who also rushed to this mega event.

Was the diet convened because of Luther?

Not at all. His case came way at the end of the order of business.

They came together to present diverse concerns to the emperor of the
Holy Roman Empire of the German Nation. However, his position was
incredibly weak because the Diet of Worms began on January 27, 1521:
Emperor Charles V had just turned twenty-one and had just recently been
elected. Many princes would have rather seen the French king Francis I
or the Englishman Henry VIII at this job. But no, it was Charles V. So
there.

Was he interested at all in the little intramural German squabbles? He
was simultaneously King of Spain and ruled over a colonial amalgama-
tion of smaller states that stretched from South America to the Philippines
("an empire on which the sun never sets"). Charles was so stressed by his
worldwide foreign policy that he let himself be represented for weeks in
Worms by his brother Ferdinand, king of Austria. The individual terri-
torial princes, of course, wanted to have more autonomous powers and
wanted to not be spoon-fed from the top and patronized. For Charles, a
strict solidarity of all the powers was severely needed: the Turks were at
that moment conquering their way to the Balkans! Therefore, an "imperial register order" was supposed to be produced in Worms, a list of the
incomes, tax rates, and defense capacities of each territory. The princes
and the imperial cities were, however, stingy. Nonetheless, Emperor
Charles still had to be divinely rich, right? His Spanish conquistadors had
amassed vast gold and silver treasures from the enslaved Incas in Peru. In
reality: he was deep in debt with those who had voted for him as emperor.

But even worse, the pope was doubly poor.

Indebted to the Fugger banking family, he had to continuously dump
new millions into his large construction project, St. Peter's Basilica. An

---

1. Saager, *Luther-Anekdoten*, 93.

emperor in a tight spot, a pope short of money, many princes in a mood for resistance—that was the situation.

Why was Luther summoned in the first place?

Good question. Officially inviting someone to the diet (and offering him a public stage) who had been declared an "un-person" and a wanted heretic was either a little taunt of the emperor's at the pope or it was a concession to the Saxon prince Frederick the Wise, who had requested a hearing.

On the evening of April 17, 1521, at six o'clock, the "shaveling" was summoned in front of the gathered assembly of men to recant his writings. "Now all of my books were lying in a row on a bench. Where they may have gotten them, I don't know. Then I said, 'Your most gracious majesty, most gracious princes and lords, the matter is important and large. I cannot answer at this time. I ask of you to grant me time to think about it.'"[2]

Say again? Luther was not well prepared?

It seems hardly possible after a fourteen-day journey. Given his audacity to stand trial the next day, he was pushing his luck. Every additional night in Worms was life-threatening: "There came many from the nobility into my lodging and said: 'Doctor, they're saying they want to burn you, but that mustn't happen, they must all perish.'"[3] Were the nobles implying that the troops of the pro-Lutheran imperial knight Franz von Sickingen would start a bloodbath if something happened to Luther?

Whether he spent the night pondering in panic, pleadingly praying, or sleeping deeply, no one knows. But on April 18, 1521, he summarized in a long speech the essential points of his three books *On the Freedom of a Christian*, *To the Christian Nobility of the German Nation*, and *On the Babylonian Captivity of the Church*. His most provocative claims were these:

1. The pope doesn't stand authoritatively *over* the Bible, but rather *under* it, and is accountable to the people of the church.

---

2. Henkys, *Luthers Tischreden*, 28.
3. Ibid.

2. Every baptized individual is called to read and interpret the Bible and to celebrate Mass. There is, therefore, a "general priesthood of the laity."
3. Every Christian must be more obedient to his or her conscience bound by the Bible than the dogmas that a council enacted.

Could Charles V have estimated the explosive power of these thoughts in the slightest? Probably not. The emperor appeared weary, and after all he could hardly speak German or go into the details. Used to being the most dominant guy in the room, all he said was: "Recant!"

And Luther answered, "If I am not convinced by the testimony of Scripture and plain reason, then I will neither believe the pope nor the councils alone because it is certain that they have erred more often and have contradicted themselves—so I am overcome in my conscience by the passages of Scripture and trapped in the Word of God. Therefore, I cannot and will not recant because it is neither safe nor healthy to act against the conscience. God help me. Amen."[4]

> "While I was speaking, they requested that I should repeat it once again in Latin. But I was really sweating a lot and was hot from half of the turmoil so that I could hardly stand under the princes."

So. Where does "Here I stand, I cannot do otherwise" come from then?

The simplest explanation: the quote was attributed to him soon thereafter while Luther was being hailed as a hero.

The most humorous explanation is: Luther actually said "I can't do any more." Many years later, he related at the table, "While I was speaking, they requested that I should repeat it once again in Latin. But I was really sweating a lot and was hot from half of the turmoil so that I could hardly stand under the princes."[5] Obviously: the room was overcrowded, the air was bad, and Luther was nervous.

"Then said Friedrich von Thun to me: 'If you could not do it, then it is enough, Doctor.' But I repeated all of my words in Latin. That pleased Duke Frederick [the Wise], the electoral prince, overall very well."[6] Also obvious: Luther's political patron wanted to be sure that the emperor had understood everything. And that the papal keepers of the minutes wrote down only the quote of Luther in Latin, please, the lingua franca. "As I had finished speaking, they let me go. And I was provided two people, who led me. There a turmoil arose. 'Where were they leading him captive?' cried the noblemen. But I said: 'They are only accompanying me.' Then I came back to my lodging and wasn't again in the imperial council."[7]

Let's consider for second: If Luther gave his speech of defense twice and said the end in Latin the second time, a later translation extracted from the word "withstand" and the phrase "I cannot and will not . . ." could have built the proverbial quote of today. Just maybe.

What did Luther unleash with his statement?

Initially, on-site and concretely, not a lot. The diet continued to discuss and to squabble on further. Emperor Charles's own excommunication of Luther (after that of the pope's) was not made until five weeks afterward and would provide much trouble eight years later as the Edict of Worms.

Centuries later, the intellectual, spiritual, clerical, and thereby political avalanches that Luther set off here became apparent. Very simply put: the man invented individualism. *Before* him many scientists and artists like Leonardo da Vinci or Michelangelo Buonarotti had already acted out of individual freedom and were protected by their genius and popularity. Now, however, a short, heavy guy from Saxony demanded these freedoms for *all people*.

The impact and the effect of this speech can hardly be overestimated: a

5. Henkys, *Luthers Tischreden*, 29.
6. Ibid.
7. Ibid.

person invoked what he had read himself (!) in the Bible and what seemed to him to be "reasonable." With that he installed his "conscious tied to Scripture" and, for him, his own thinking as the highest moral authority! He called for allowing individuals to believe, think, and reason independently, and afterward the freedom to act accordingly. Martin Luther claimed that the human being is the direct and personal counterpart of God, that he or she may demand spiritual freedom (and, as a logical consequence, the freedom of science and art, freedom of the press, freedom of conscience, freedom of religion, freedom of assembly, and freedom of expression), and that one can accept the moral responsibility for his or her actions.

The right to say "no" and the obligation to have to say "no"—with these, the spiritual twins of *freedom* and *responsibility* came into the world. The foundation for the ideas of humankind for the following centuries. The foundation for each humane legal system. The signal for the emancipation of the individual.

Where did Luther get that from?

Good question. From his profound knowledge of the Bible, perhaps? There is Job, who referred to his faith and experience of life to persistently contradict the steadfast dogma "sickness is the punishment for sin." Jesus, who confronted the teaching of the priests and told the Pharisees, "The Sabbath was made for man, not man for the Sabbath" (Mark 2:27). There were the disciples of Jesus, Peter and John, who received a ban on speaking and said to the religious court, "Which is right in God's eyes: to listen to you, or to him?" (Acts 4:19). Paul, who was charged by a Roman court as an insurrectionist and defended his transformation from persecutor of Christians to confessor of Christ (Acts 26:2–29).

What we do know is that Martin Luther often reflected on the former rector of the University of Prague, Jan Hus (1369–1415), who preached a freedom of conscience and a "general priesthood" and had also written from his conscience. And was burned at the stake on July 6, 1415, at the council in Constance, Germany.

The poet Heinrich Heine wrote three hundred years later, "When

Luther spoke out the sentence that one must refute his teachings only through the Bible itself or through sound reason, human rationality was granted the right to interpret the Bible. Through this arose the freedom of conscience in Germany, and the authority of reason became legitimate."[8]

Another hundred years later, the otherwise critical-of-Luther novelist Thomas Mann went so far as to claim, "While he established the immediacy of the relation of mankind to their God, he advanced the European democracy in that 'every man is his own priest,' that is democracy. The German idealistic philosophy, the refinement of psychology through pietistic soul-searching, . . . this comes from Luther."[9]

If one wants to divide the history of Europe into epochs, one can say: in Worms, on April 18, 1521, the Middle Ages ended. Whether the modern era began there or with the French Revolution in 1789, whether it was Martin Luther or rather Immanuel Kant who began the Enlightenment— those questions are still open to debate.

The individual's absolute sovereignty and the loosing of church and state control over the consciences of the people definitely begins *here*. At the Diet in Worms. Even without a "Here I stand."

---

8. Heine, *Sämtliche Werke*, 25.
9. Renner, *Klassiker deutschen Denkens*, 303.

Chapter 13

Luther's Most Important Insight Came While He Was on the Toilet

In truth, Luther sat there less often than he would have liked, but there is a long-standing myth that he discovered the foundational truth of the Reformation while reclused in necessary privacy. He described his theological breakthrough as a classic eureka moment: "All at once I felt that I had been born again and entered into paradise itself through open gates. Immediately I saw the whole of Scripture in a different light."[1] *When* this happened is up for grabs—a fixed date for his so-called tower experience on the peaceful privy is nowhere to be found. *Where* this happened is also not settled. But, even more importantly, *what* exactly happened to change Luther's thinking?

A twenty-three-year-old Martin woke up at three in the morning at the monastery in Erfurt to say the morning prayer. The times of prayer followed in three hour increments, there was little and simple food, the cells were cold, and the accommodations were purposely kept humble—everything ordered to help a monk master impulses and desires and to demonstrate to God a "complacent life." Luther hoped to experience a pleasing union of the human soul with God through asceticism and contemplation. He felt,

---

1. Luther, *The Complete Edition of Luther's Latin Works (1545)*, 421–28.

however, an ever-widening gap between the imperfect yet seeking human and the everlasting, all-powerful, exalted God.

The young monk was convinced humans were called to perfection. He observed, however: no one achieves this. Never. Because humans make mistakes, they desire the wrong things and cause evil. In short: because we are sinners. And one can only confess and atone for so much to the angry, demanding, bossy God—still that will never be enough. "I had confessed my guilt again and again, and the punishment, which I had to do for penance, I performed willingly. But nevertheless I never received the desired certainty."[2]

The desired certainty was: God loves me, accepts me, forgives my sins, and pulls me out of a never-ending spiral of new regret, confession, penitential exercises, and good works that make me proud of my merit. Pride and vanity are, however, once again the next sins, and so starts the circus of contrition from the beginning.

When Luther came to the monastery in Wittenberg at age twenty-seven, he came to know there a fatherly friend: the cofounder of the university and its pastor, Johann von Staupitz (1468–1524). He assured Luther, "God is not angry with you, Martinus, you are angry with God!"[3] One could almost take this to be, in the modern sense, psychotherapeutic. Staupitz encouraged Luther that rather than mulling over self-perfection on earth and eternal bliss in heaven ("How do I get to a merciful God?") he should instead write a tangible doctoral thesis: "Then you would have a task." And he advised him "to contemplate the man, whose name is Christ!"[4] Christ stands between the perfect, eternal, exalted, unreachable God and imperfect, mortal, wicked human beings. His death on the cross fully makes up for the shortcomings of man before God.

Luther finished his doctorate, received the university's chair of theology, and held lectures on the Psalms in the winter semester of 1513. Two years later he lectured on Romans. In doing so he stumbled upon Romans

---

2. Mayer, *Martin Luther*, 29.
3. Ibid., 28.
4. Ibid., 39.

1:17: "For in the gospel the righteousness of God is revealed—a righteousness that is by faith from first to last, just as it is written: 'The righteous
will live by faith.'" In response, Luther exclaimed, "At last! After days
and nights of contemplation, it came to me. Now I understand what the
righteousness of God means: it is the gift that makes mankind righteous!
Before you make Christ your role model and example for life, you must
accept and recognize him as an offering and gift, which is given to you
from God and is supposed to belong to you."[5]

> "At last! After days and nights of contemplation,
> it came to me. Now I understand what the
> righteousness of God means."

Therefore, it is not religious, moral efforts that make people the beloved
children of God, but God—from himself and out of love—came into the
world through Jesus Christ and reconciled the world with the demands of
his commandments. How? Through Christ as his representative he par-
dons and forgives what no person could ever make right or atone for.
Grace comes from God's love and is "mercifully fair" and brings about a
relationship of affectionate faith between humanity and God. This, then,
is the *what* of Luther's discovery.

When, exactly, these thoughts came to Luther is disputed by scholars.
Because he spoke of an "epiphany" in his study in the southern tower of
the Augustinian monastery in Wittenberg, many assume an isolated aha
"tower experience" sometime between his arrival in Wittenberg in 1511
and his lecture on the book of Romans in 1515. But because Luther also
said, "through writing, reading, and learning, I've increasingly gained
my insights,"[6] other scholars assume a step-by-step spiritual development
until 1518.

---

5. Ibid., 43, 49.
6. Ibid., 40.

What about the *where*, the story that these insights came while he was in the privy?

In his preface to his Latin works from 1545, Luther spoke of his years-long reflection on the term "justification of sinners." In Johannes Aurifaber's record of Luther's table talks, the addendum *super cloacam* appeared in this context—which one should not translate as "super toilet," but instead it means "above the sewage" or also "despite nasty odors." This notation in the much later *Table Talks* accounts for the origin of the idea that Luther had his great insight while actually on the toilet. But it is also possible that the older Luther took a bit of mischievous delight in tweaking the ears of his hearers. Potty language was rather the norm for the times, a fact that negates those looking for some psychological significance here.

One explanation is that Luther was referring to his personal study in the *cloaca* tower of the monastery, a heated office on the third floor with a toilet on the lower level. Other scholars note that *in cloaca* was a term familiar to medieval monks. It described a vulnerable state of being under demonic attack, a *cloaca* being a place of filth and all things ungodly.[7]

Another possible explanation: since the growing fame of his Ninety-Five Theses against the abuse of confession and indulgences in the winter of 1517–18, a smear campaign was carried out against Luther and his works. Very simply: whatever he wrote was indeed crap! Later, opponents vilified the texts themselves: whoever dispenses with the judgment of God and the demanded penances so simply is in reality a—brace yourself—"cowardly crapper in his pants," as the German says. Obviously his critics were, as we say today, taking the low road. But as already noted, such crude vitriol was common usage for the times (and was used even by Luther himself!). So perhaps his theological insights were gained *despite* the vulgarities thrown his way.

Luther's opponents had a field day when his stomach and bowel pains were made known, which Luther himself moaned about in letters to Philip Melanchthon. (Alert! Squeamish readers may skip down further

---

7. Oberman, *Luther*, 155.

in the text.) On May 12, 1521, he wrote, "My stool is so hard that I'm forced to thrust it out with such energy until I break a sweat. Yesterday, I excreted once after four days. As a consequence, I didn't sleep the entire night. Please pray for me because this malady is becoming unbearable."[8] Anyone who has suffered from similarly severe constipation can sympathize. Surprisingly to us today, there was already a "tabloid newspaper" five hundred years ago that broadcasted such unfortunate personal details about Luther with relish!

Another friend, George Spalatin, sent him natural medicinal pellets, and Luther thanked him: "I've now received everything and tried as instructed and shortly afterward purged without blood and violent pushing."[9] Unfortunately, Spalatin's pills apparently didn't last very long. On September 9, 1521, Luther wrote: "Today, I finally had a stool after six days but it almost squeezed out my soul. Now I'm sitting here with pain like a birth mother: torn open, bruised, and bloody. When something goes again after four days, the injury starts new again. I'm still drowsy and sluggish, so much so that it gives me displeasure and makes me grumpy."[10]

So what is the best conclusion concerning Luther's tower experience? It never happened. The fallacy of those who connect his alimentary troubles with his theology is this: Luther first had stomach, bowel, and sphincter illnesses when he was thirty-eight years old. At that point, his aha tower experience of the justification of sinners had long since been formulated.

That Luther had a convenient privy available is now beyond doubt. In October 2004 German archaeologists discovered his lavatory in an annex in his house in Wittenberg. It includes a vaulted ceiling, late-Gothic sandstone doorframes, and what is left of a floor-heating system, which presumably gave Luther an added bit of comfort during the hours he spent in contemplation. "This is a great find," said Stefan Rhein, the director of the Luther Memorial Foundation. Professor Rhein said the foundation would

---

8. Luther, *D. Martin Luther's Werke*, vol. 1, chap. 2, 1–2.
9. Ibid., 16.
10. Ibid., 8.

stop any of the eighty thousand annual visitors to Wittenberg, who come in search of the spirit of Luther, from sitting on the toilet. "I would not sit on it. There's a point where you have to draw the line."[11]

We completely agree.

---

11. "Toilet Where Luther Strained to Produce the Reformation," *Sydney Morning Herald*.

Chapter 14

Luther Was a Warmonger

The idea that Luther was a bloodthirsty warmonger is thoroughly false. The myth arose from an incoherent Luther quote, written as an open letter to every prince of the various realms during the chaos of the peasants' revolts: "Let whoever can, stab, smite, slay. If you die in the process, good for you! A more blessed death you cannot experience because you die in obeying God's command."[1] Nowadays, it's only radical Islamic terrorists who talk like that.

What in the world was going on?

Consider Germany in the 1520s: there were about 350 small state territories with an estimated fifteen million inhabitants. Approximately 75 percent of them lived off the land, and the majority were farmers. But only a minority cultivated their *own* land. The rest belonged to the aristocratic families, princes, counts, dukes, knights, bishops, abbots, councilmen, and rich citizens. They had developed an economic system based on medieval feudalism in which fiefs (the peasant class) worked the land based on a complex web of leases, payment-in-kind deals, levies, customs, and income taxes. It worked well so long as no wages needed to be paid.

The farmhands were not "employed" in the modern sense but were

---

1. Mayer, *Martin Luther*, 126.

"bond servants." That is, they were *bonded* to the capital assets of the landowners or leaseholders. Subjectively, the farmers were free. They were self-supporters and could, theoretically, live off the profit margin between the production costs and market price of their products. But objectively and de facto they were not free at all. They were dependent on how much interest, redemption, and tax they or their feudal lords had to pay on the land, living quarters, agricultural buildings, farm animals, plants, and tools. Next to these bond servants, there were farmers, who from the murky past were ancestral "serfs." They were bound to a plot of land by heredity, served their lords by working the land and giving them a substantial portion of the goods produced. That didn't hinder their masters, however, from also demanding a high tax on the serfs' own share of their harvest.

But when bad harvests came into play, epidemic influenza, or pests (as they did in 1501–1502 in southern Germany), then the children starved to death, the women prostituted themselves, and the men went into debt to each other. Some knights, who stopped by as taxmen commissioned by the princes, were fetched from their horses and hanged. Or hacked to pieces. Or burned alive. Then, as now, no one likes the taxman.

Bundschuh, or "drawstring shoes," is what the rebels called themselves. This was a self-deprecating contrast between the serfs' hand-laced shoes and the riding boots of the knights. When the bishop of Speyer merely heard of a planned revolt of seven thousand farmers in and around Bruchsal (he only heard of it, mind you), he ordered ten of them to be quartered, which means having each arm and leg ripped off by a coach horse and then hanging the torsos out along the streets. Every once in a while until 1517, regional Bundschuh rebellions flared up in various areas of Germany.

Against the later idealization of the peasant farmers by the communist government of the former East Germany, it is only fair to note: the lynch law of the furious farmers befell not only the nobles in the land but also *Jewish* merchants and moneylenders in the cities.

It was in this political atmosphere that Luther's writings were spread among the people: *On the Freedom of a Christian*, *To the Christian Nobility of the German Nation*, and *Concerning the Monk's Vow*. The pious theology professor from Wittenberg acted like a spark in a powder keg. The gunpowder exploded. Not only did the farmers have their hardships and economic injustices as legitimation and motivation, but now they also fought for the gospel, for the true faith, against a decadent, corrupt pope and church!

A few years later, in 1523, Martin Luther reaffirmed to George Spalatin, "I never intended to incite disobedience, disunity, and revolt. I want only this: to serve God's Word and glory through my speaking and writing and to promote the faith and neighborly love.[2]

The rebels, however, met these platitudes with knives and torches in their hands. No, no, Professor Luther, instead of good-hearted motives, the farmers drafted concrete political demands. "Twelve Articles of the Peasants in Swabia," their written response was called. Abolishment of serfdom. Changed usage rights for agriculture, forestry, and hunting. New rules for interest and repayment with loan agreements. A voice in taxation. Voting for the minister by the congregation. Distribution of free church property to the needy. And so on.

What seems to us to be a mild labor union program was, for a theocratic-hierarchical society, pure anarchy. Already from 1517 onward, the intellectual, spiritual, and moral columns of the world were crumbling. Now, uneducated farmers were sawing down the legal and military pillars of the social order. They went about this quite "enthusiastically": plundering monasteries, raping nuns, ravaging churches, besieging villages, and setting fire to castles. Out of fear of the hordes, some cities fought, of necessity, on their side. Luther traveled through Thuringia and was horrified: "I was in mortal danger amid the rebellious farmers."[3]

In April 1525, he printed *Admonition to Peace*. To the peasants he wrote, "You don't want to bear that one inflicts injury and injustice on you. You want to be free and have property and your full rights. But Christ says one should put up no resistance to evil and injustice. If you don't want to

---

2. Ibid., 121.
3. Ibid., 125.

hold to this, then you should not claim the title 'Christian' for yourselves. It worries me that several prophets of death have fallen into your ranks."[4]

Luther hardly goes into detail in his *Admonition* regarding the political demands of the peasants. Why not? Because he's a cowardly "prince toady," as revolutionary thinkers, left-wing politicians, and human-rights activists have said for centuries? Or because he simply didn't have any political ideas and the peasants didn't have any either? Which form of rule or government was supposed to come after the elimination of the existing form?

From such confusion, the socialist politician and Karl Marx biographer Franz Mehran (1846–1919) wondered to himself:

> How infinitely little the "great" Luther proves with respect to the great questions of his time! What did he have to say concerning the twelve articles of the peasants, which today nobody still contests? Nothing more than empty sayings. He rejected the abolition of serfdom "because Abraham also had servants"! The Old Testament "tithe" as a measure for taxes impressed him so much that he labeled the amounts of the peasants after allowance as "nothing but plunder and bush theft"![5]

Luther's concept of the "two rules"—the earthly rule of humanity and the heavenly kingdom of God in the afterlife—meant for him that the freedom of a Christian consisted solely of being acquitted through Christ through God's forgiveness of sinners—"A Christian man is the most free lord of all, and subject to none." Civic or even revolutionary "freedom" is not meant for this life. On the contrary, here "a Christian man is the most dutiful servant of all, and subject to everyone."[6]

For Luther, there is no Christian justification for or right of resistance. "There is no authority," as he understood in Paul's letter to the Christians

---

4. Ibid., 123.
5. Mehring, *Gesammelte Schriften*, 250–51.
6. Luther, *First Principles of the Reformation*, 104.

in Rome, "except that which God has established. . . . Whoever rebels against the authority is rebelling against what God has instituted" (Rom. 13:1–2). Period.

That Luther religiously justifies the dull suffering of disenfranchised workers for the following centuries, thus programming in the typical Prussian-Protestant blind obedience; that he inevitably triggered the disappointment and contempt of the social reformers of the eighteenth and nineteenth centuries, and the Communists' hate and fury toward Christians in the twentieth-century—can or *must* one retrospectively reproach Luther?

> "Once the bloodshed begins, it doesn't cease so quickly. There is then only an end with terror."

He wrote this to the princes: "What use is it then, when the field of a farmer would yield so many pieces of gold such as stalks and grains, but the lordship only ever demands more in order to increase their gluttony! The poor man cannot and will not bear it any longer! Once the bloodshed begins, it doesn't cease so quickly. There is then only an end with terror."[7]

Apart from the fact that this writing is the origin of the colloquial German idiom "end with terror," Luther's call to peace was thin, lukewarm, and came too late.

"The peasants' revolt, if it had prevailed—evangelically inspired, as it was—could have given the entire German history a happy turn toward freedom. Luther, however, hated it because he saw in it nothing but a desolate compromise of his work on spiritual liberation and therefore cursed and mocked the revolt," the writer Thomas Mann regretted. "Luther was both great and German in his ambiguity as a liberating and, at the same time, a reactionary force. He was a conservative revolutionary."[8]

---

7.   Mayer, *Martin Luther*, 124.
8.   Renner, *Klassiker deutschen Denkens*, 303.

On May 14–15, 1525, around six thousand well-armed soldiers under the strategically smart leadership of Philip I, landgrave of Hesse, defeated approximately eight thousand disorganized peasants, who lined up with flails, scythes, and pitchforks. The Battle of Frankenhausen was militarily not a peasants' war—it was a massacre.

Shortly before, Luther added to his work *Admonition to Peace* the line, "*Also* against the murderous, thieving hordes of the *other* peasants."[9] In his criticism, he wanted to distinguish between the anarchist peasants and those ready to negotiate, but in the heated mood of the times, many publishers only printed the second part of the pamphlet and thus needed to simplify the title. So it became: *Against the Murderous, Thieving Hordes of Peasants.* By the time the paper reached readers, the peasants' revolt was subdued all over Germany.

Had Luther, as a warmonger, already instigated the slaughter at Frankenhausen? No, that would be an incorrect backdating of history, in my opinion.

---

9. Kunst, *Luther und der Krieg*, 20.

Chapter 15

Luther Did Not Want to Translate the Old Testament into German

Of course he did. But he didn't have the time to do all the Bible from front to back, as it were. He also didn't have much time to concentrate on translating the Old Testament. And he knew it was a task beyond his capabilities alone.

Already in January 1522 in the Wartburg hideout, he moaned in a letter, "With this [the New Testament], I've brought a great burden upon myself, which goes beyond my strength. Now I see what interpreting means and why nobody until now has tried. . . . I won't touch the Old Testament if you all are not here and contribute."[1]

And it remained so. Even before the German New Testament (the "September Bible" of 1522) was published, Luther had already put together a team of linguists, theologians, and secretaries for the OT: Philip Melanchthon, obviously; the Hebrew experts Johann Forster, Bernhard Ziegler, and Matthäus Aurogallus; his university colleague Nicolaus von Amsdorf from the philosophy department; the pastors Georg Rörer and Johannes Bugenhagen as clerks; his friend Justus Jonas; and finally Caspar Cruciger as editor.

---

1. Köthe, *Martin Luther und Luthergedenkstätten*, 104.

There were no smartphones so no one snapped selfies—but the son of the painter Lucas Cranach, Lucas Cranach the Younger, squeezed nine of these ten gentlemen into a single painting.

But because Luther's attention and time were taken up by radical religious "enthusiasts," by the political firestorm of the peasants' revolts against the princes, by a certain Katharina von Bora, by family circumstances, by the Eucharistic controversy, by the Diet of Augsburg, and by the continual composition of new essays, it took twelve years (!) until this Wittenberg dream team could finally release their monumental opus, *Biblia, That Is the Entire Holy Scripture in German*, in the summer of 1534. Melchior Lotter the Younger was allowed to print it this time (he had done the New Testament), but it was his competitor Hans Lufft who later took over the project and delivered a hundred thousand copies in the following decades.

As an aside, I still marvel at where population numbers in history books come from. In the Middle Ages, for example, the birthrate was high, but infant mortality was too. Pests and regional wars carried off millions, but great currents of refugees poured into the depopulated villages again. And despite all that there wasn't a registration office to keep track of numbers. But that "every third adult in the middle of the sixteenth century owned a Luther Bible"[2] seems probable. A few years after publication, idioms and words became fixed in the vernacular that were first "invented" by Martin Luther: *feuertaufe* (litmus test), *bluthund* (bloodhound), *selbstverleugnung* (self-denial), *machtwort* (decree), *schandfleck* (eyesore), *lückenbüßer* (a person who is a stopgap), *gewissensbisse* (remorse), *lästermaul* (scandalmonger), *lockvogel* (decoy bird), *"Perlen vor die Säue werfen"* (to cast pearls before swine), *"ein Buch mit sieben Siegeln"* (to be a closed book), *"im Dunkeln tappen"* (to grope in the dark), *"ein Herz und eine Seele"* (to be one heart and one soul), *"auf Sand bauen"* (to build on sand), *"Wolf im Schafspelz"* (a wolf in sheep's clothing), and *"der große Unbekannte"* (the great unknown)—all go back to Luther.[3]

---

2. Möller, *Deutschland im Zeitalter der Reformation*, 90.
3. Van Flocken, "Wie Luthers Bibel unsere Sprache prägt."

Did Martin have less passion for the Old Testament than for the New Testament because it does indeed have endless genealogies, countless retold stories, and detailed Jewish religious rules?

"One is not allowed to despise the Old Testament," warned Luther. "One must read it indeed thoroughly. Here you will find the diapers and the manger in which Christ laid."[4] What he meant is that one only understands the Old Testament correctly when it is read as a pre-text and pointer to Jesus Christ. We are only able to decipher it *through* Christ. The question has been under discussion among Christians for over five hundred years: Is the (partly gruesome and seemingly contradictory) Old Testament also "God's Word"?

Luther said: "Yes, but." Yes, but God's "Word became Scripture" is interpreted correctly through God's "Word became flesh." That means: no ban in the Old Testament can or may be applied that supersedes Christ or interpreted as if there hadn't been Jesus and his teachings, his life, death, and resurrection. Measured and weighed, inherited as binding or left as era-specific, everything in the OT comes with the help of a determining benchmark: Christ!

For Luther, being obedient to God didn't mean meticulously following every rule of the Old Testament or taking all possible verses verbatim. Being obedient to God means: faith in Christ. To trust in him, his being, his conduct, his sentiments. To follow his example. And when some ultra fundamentalist sects (who hold that each word of the Bible was dictated by God without contradiction, so the Old Testament law is binding today) point to the fact that Jesus, as a practicing Jew, was bound to the Old Testament, Luther would answer them, "Be careful that you don't make a Moses out of Christ, a Torah out of the gospel, as it has thus far always been."[5]

So, is it worth reading the OT at all?

And how! Luther's groundbreaking "new" thoughts, which changed everything from 1517 onward—the German language, the church, soci-

---

4. Mayer, *Martin Luther*, 112.
5. Ibid.

ety, politics, worldview, and Western philosophy to this day—didn't come to him simply overnight, but were largely prepared through lectures on the Psalms at the University of Wittenberg during the winter semester of 1513. Psalms of thanksgiving, sorrow, and even the difficult imprecatory Psalms.

"Be careful that you don't make a Moses out of Christ, a Torah out of the gospel, as it has thus far always been."

Also in dealing with the Old Testament, the Hebrew Bible, Luther showed on the one hand a holy reverence for the text and on the other hand an unconcerned freedom to innovate: the first two books of Maccabees, the book of Judith, the book of Tobit, the book of Sirach, the Wisdom of Solomon, and others he separated without hesitation (and dropped 1 and 2 Esdras completely). He found them not so important. And it was named the "Apocrypha" after all.[6] It is for this reason that even today Catholics, who kept them, have a thicker Bible than Protestants.

Luther's image of the Old Testament is that of a forest: "The Holy Scriptures is like a very vast and wide forest, in which many trees of all kinds stand, from which one can break many fruits. One has in the Bible a wealth of comfort, doctrine, instruction, admonition, warning, promise, and threat. There is not one single large tree in this forest on which I didn't knock, and a few apple or pear trees from which I have broken off or shook some fruit."[7]

---

6. The Greek word means "hidden," but the books themselves have a long (and debated) history. Luther was the first to place the Apocrypha between the Testaments. The Puritans dropped them from the Bible completely while the Roman Catholic Church retained them as deuterocanonical Scripture.

7. Krumbholz, *Euch stoßen,* 19.

Chapter 16

Luther Was the First Lutheran

Believe it or not, the first person to be called a Lutheran became a folk hero in the German Democratic Republic (the now defunct communist East Germany), and his picture graced one of its currency bills. Oddly enough, that person was not Martin Luther. No. The first person to be called a "Lutheran" was twenty-nine-year-old Thomas Müntzer. In 1518 he carried the name proudly at first—later not at all.

Thomas Müntzer—almost everyone in the "good old GDR" knew him. Around two hundred agricultural cooperatives were named "LPG Thomas Müntzer." Groups of the state youth organization, the Free German Youth, carried his name, and even troops of the national people's army had the Thomas Müntzer Brigade. Every GDR citizen had his image already in hand on the five-mark bill. The first "Lutheran" was the only theologian to ever adorn the banknote of a communist state.

"How did that happen?" one rightly wonders.

Thomas, as the son of a coiner, studied law, medicine, and theology, was ordained as a (Catholic) priest in 1514—and was convinced in 1518 to accept Luther's reform proposals. In his next position, he had a falling out with the Franciscan monks, and in the following position, he supported the rebellious cloth manufactures and weavers. Such escapades caused scandal with church and city authorities. In 1521 he fled by night and fog from Zwickau to Prague. He named his fellow priests and monks (Caution! "Colorful language" to follow.) "damned villains, devilish servants, a plague of the poor people, usury-addicted, interest-excited clerics, whore-stallions, and calf milk bastards, foolish straw-like teachers and scrotum doctors."[1] Speaking, no doubt, in all Christian charity.

He certainly could call a spade a spade, as well as other names. It is quite fitting, then, that he signed documents with "Thomas Müntzer with his hammer." He had a concrete conception of people by which he oriented himself: the simple, pious laity were the "real followers of Jesus Christ" versus the rest. He saw this ideal type embodied in the rebellious worker and peasants. An outer reversal must follow the inner conversion process of an individual, Müntzer thought. Because one cannot divide humanity into a spiritual part and a physical part, the healing process between God and humanity must lead to a healing process between worldly king and subject. The kingdom of God in heart and heaven needs an equivalent in the "kingdom of this world." Müntzer saw an example of this in the shared property of the first Christians in Jerusalem: "All the believers were together and had everything in common. They sold property and possessions to give to anyone who had need. Every day they continued to meet together in the temple courts. They broke bread in their homes and ate together with glad and sincere hearts" (Acts 2:44–46).

The church authorities—the Catholics as it happened, but unfortunately also the not-yet-Lutherans as well—held this to be an infatuation (we would call it social romanticism) that bode ill for Müntzer. For his part, he believed they had betrayed Christ and his gospel and "no supposedly anointed cleric and spiritual appearing monk can declare the reason for faith in the very finest dust."[2]

He performed the Mass completely in the German language, and so it is no wonder that multitudes of the poor and the oppressed of society especially flocked to Müntzer's flaming sermons. When Count Ernst von

---

1. Vogler, *Thomas Müntzer*, 107.
2. Ellinger, *Thomas Müntzer*, 56–57.

Mansfeld (who was friends with Luther's parents) forbade such rebellious actions, Müntzer wrote to him: "I will regard you as pranksters, villains, scoundrels, and heathens. If you wanted to stop the course of the gospel, the sword will be taken from you and the spirit will empower a regiment, which cannot be overturned by a loose cannon."[3]

The "sword"—that is, the legislative, police, and judicial powers—in the hands of the people? Spiritual resistance, which no gunpowder can break? In a single sentence, Thomas Müntzer had formulated the thought of the *sovereign people*—the foundation of every modern democracy—and the right to civil disobedience on grounds of conscience.

He was already disappointed by Luther's Reformation, even though it was still in full swing. For the social and economic conditions of the simple people, it had no effect; for the nobility, it worked quite well, Müntzer thought. The peasant class fully agreed and posed the simple but radical statement, "All of God's commandments and the practices of the apostles are now supposed to be followed, except for one: the communion of goods. And the equality of all people."[4] Why not?

And Luther? Luther countered with an inflammatory pamphlet, "*Letter to the Princes of Saxony Concerning the Rebellious Spirit*," and the work doesn't belong among the glorious chapters of the reformer: "Müntzer, the archdevil who causes robbery, murder, and bloodshed, has been ostracized by the emperor and God, so that whoever can and would like to strangle the same one should rightly do so."[5] Ouch. As they say, politics (and in this case, religion) isn't tiddlywinks.

How quickly indeed does a persecuted heretic become a persecuting hunter of heretics. Luther uttered what Islamists today call a *fatwa*, an incitement to murder. "The devil doesn't make the body and possessions free, only the soul does! Also, the gospel doesn't make all goods in common, but only thee, who freely do such, as the apostle and disciples did. They didn't demand the foreign goods of Pilate and Herod to be common,

3. Ibid., 384.
4. Goertz, *Thomas Müntzer*, 36.
5. Luther, *D. Martin Luther's Werke*, vol. 18, 357.

like our senseless peasants clamored, but instead to have only their own goods common!"[6]

Five hundred years later, theologians are still trying to grapple with this idea: Is the gospel just about salvation or is it also about physical well-being? Is it just about the justification of sinners in heaven or also about justice for sinners on earth? Does the church just teach prayer or also physical resistance? Is the church to be concerned with economic and sociopolitical questions, and does it even have to be in the name of Jesus? Or does politics have nothing to do with the pulpit?

> "Müntzer, the archdevil . . . whoever can and would
> like to strangle the same one should rightly do so."

Ironically enough, it was the socially engaged Pietists of the nineteenth century and the poor Catholic priests of the twentieth century who stood closer to Thomas Müntzer than they did to Martin Luther!

The early bird catches the worm? Right. But he chokes on it if he sings too soon: two-hundred and fifty years before the French Revolution and four hundred years before the Communist Revolution in Russia, Müntzer didn't want anything less than the socialization of the means of production. He answered Luther, calling it "the deeply provoked discourse of protection against the spiritless, mildly-living body in Wittenberg," in which he rebutted the charge of insurrection with the letter that he openly distributed on July 1, 1524, to Johann, Elector of Saxony, stating that "an entire community has the force of the sword."[7]

That didn't make the duke happy. Democracy? As unimaginable as a jumbo jet on the village street in 1524! But Müntzer was thinking in terms of logical consequence: what Luther had initiated as a disempowerment of the bishops in favor of a general priesthood of the laity, he now

---

6. Bornkamm and Ebeling, *Martin Luther,* vol. 4, 135.
7. Vogler, *Thomas Müntzer,* 218.

wanted to carry on as a disempowerment of the princes in favor of a governance of the people:

> Nevertheless comes Father Soft-Step, alas, the compliant fellow, and says, "I wanted to start a rebellion." Luther says, "The princes should confidently strike the thieves and robbers." He doesn't disclose, however, the sources of all thievery: look here, the source of the evil of usury and robbery are our lords and princes! They take all creatures as their property: the fish in the sea, the birds in the air, the plants in the soil—all must be theirs! Only then do they institute God's commandment and they say to the poor, "You shall not steal." Thus, they flay and scrape the poor plowman, workman, and everyone who lives there—thus, he who abducts the very least, he must be hanged. To this the Wittenberger Dr. Liar says "Amen!" The lords do the same in that the poor man becomes their enemy. They don't want to put aside the cause of the revolt. Because I say this, I must be incendiary, indeed![8]

Even five hundred years later, Müntzer's claims engage the United Nations General Assembly in New York, the International Court of Justice in The Hague, governments all over the world, countless environmental and human-rights organizations, church federations, and Christian charities: To whom belongs the water and air? Who acquires the land and from whom and for how long? To whom belongs the usage rights of natural resources and raw materials? Or on a smaller scale: since the 2008 financial crisis, the words "bank robber" no longer mean men in stocking masks with guns but rather the ones in pinstripe suits on the exchange floor. "The little ones are hung; the big ones are allowed to run"—a proverbial saying from the "first Lutheran," Thomas Müntzer. Still true today.

The first Lutherans dreamed of a democratic theocracy?

And how! Müntzer was not only inspired by his sense of justice and

---

8. Franz and Kirn, *Thomas Müntzer*, 329.

solidarity with the poor but also by the apocalyptic writings of the Bible and by church history: the books Daniel and Ezekiel in the Old Testament, the book of Revelation in the New Testament, and the early medieval mystics. Daniel 7:26–27 especially appealed to him: "But the court will sit, and his power will be taken away and completely destroyed forever. Then the sovereignty, power and greatness of all the kingdoms under heaven will be handed over to the holy people of the Most High. His kingdom will be an everlasting kingdom, and all rulers will worship and obey him."

"The little ones are hung; the big ones are allowed to run." —Thomas Müntzer

The prophecy was fulfilling itself, Müntzer thought, as he traveled in southwest Germany and was inspired by the rebellious peasants of the Bundschuh movement. Back home in Thuringia, he heard of partial regional victories of the peasants and believed that he recognized the eschatological battle between Satan and the second coming of Christ. Under a white banner with a rainbow—a symbol of innocence and God's faithfulness—Father Müntzer marched at the forefront of the peasant army moving out of Mühlhausen on April 26, 1525: "Begin! The peasants in Klettgau and Hegau of the Black Forest are up. Three thousand strong and the longer, the larger the group becomes. Strike! Now, now! While the fire is hot. Don't let your swords become cold. Forge the sword on the anvil of Nimrod.[9] Throw their tower to the ground. Now, now, while you still have time. God is leading you!"[10]

The dream of an early Christian brotherhood of communal property shared among Christ's real followers, to whom the returning Lord would bring victory in an end-times battle, lasted, sadly, only fourteen days.

9. Great-grandson of Noah, "the first tyrant on earth"; see Genesis 10:8.
10. Vogler, *Thomas Müntzer*, 244.

The army of Philip I, landgrave of Hesse, surrounded the rebels on a mountain near Frankenhausen and made them an offer: safe conduct for those who were "evilly misled" if they turned in their ringleaders. Just then, over the camp at the foot of the mountain, there appeared a colorful form: a solar halo around the setting sun. With a little imagination, it seemed to be exactly the same rainbow Thomas Müntzer had on his banner!

The meteorological display affected the peasants like an adrenaline rush. Never would they deliver their preacher and prophet to the knife![11] The prince's solders used this awe-striking moment for a surprise attack. Within two days six thousand rebels were killed. Thomas Müntzer fled inside the city wall of Frankenhausen to the attic of a house at the Anger Gate. He was discovered there by a servant of the Hessian aristocrat Otto von Eppe and was identified by means of a letter that he carried with himself. As was common practice of mercenaries, the captive was turned over to George, Duke of Saxony, as "war booty." For ten days Müntzer was interrogated and tortured, and on May 27, 1525, he was beheaded in front of the gates of Mühlhausen. His head "was laid at the crossroads at Schadeberg Keep, where one goes to Bollstedt."[12]

Müntzer's head on a pike—which was meant as a deterrent—turned out to be a pilgrimage site in the following years. Martin Luther regretted that the path there remained well trodden for a long time.[13]

And the GDR communist leadership?

Erich Honecker, dictatorial ruler of the GDR, obviously didn't fully understand Müntzer's problematic demand for an evangelical-democratic theocracy. In 1989, in a speech praising the soon to be unveiled German Peasants' War monument in Frankenhausen, as reported in *Neues Deutschland*, the Communist party newspaper, "In the fortieth year of its founding, the German Democratic Republic honors Thomas Müntzer, in appreciation for the victory over the exploiting class and the beginnings

---

11. Bensing, *Thomas Müntzer und der Thüringer Aufstand*, 225.
12. Ellinger, *Thomas Müntzer*, 821.
13. Ibid.

of the developed socialist society to fulfill the bequest of all revolutionary forces."[14]

And in another of history's great ironies, only eight weeks after the monument was opened, the Berlin Wall fell and it was the end of the socialist society once envisioned by the first Lutheran.

---

14. Transcript of South German Radio 3, June 17, 1989, 8.05 a.m., rebroadcast on May 25, 1990.

Chapter 17

Luther Wanted to Make a Name for Himself

Another myth—which was already inevitable during his own lifetime. "I ask for no one to say anything of my name, and do not name it 'Lutheran' but 'Christian'! What is Luther? Indeed, the teachings are not mine, and I wasn't crucified for anyone. How then did a stinky bag of worms [Luther] come around to saying that one should honor the children of Christ with his unholy name!"[1] That sounds modest, but it assumes Luther was already well aware of his star status in the religious firmament.

Whether men shoot the breeze around the tavern table or women whisper to each other at the market, their gossip requires heroes and villains. People that one can venerate and people that one can despise. And if a little of both could be in one and the same person—all the better! It's not any different today. Since at least the medieval (and likely) legendary Robin Hood ("a crook, but at least a good crook"), there has been an attitude of official disapproval yet secret sympathy. Examples from popular entertainment abound. Much of the appeal of rap music comes from its appeal to the "in ya face" swagger of its purveyors. Tsk, tsk, those lyrics

---

1. Luther, *D. Martin Luther's Werke*, vol. 8, 637.

are horrible! (And so catchy.) NASCAR has appealed quite openly to its roots in Prohibition and the slick-driving bootleggers who outran the law. Fans love to hate the outlaw driver, and some fans hate to love the good guys. Sure, the legendary D. B. Cooper held a passenger plane hostage and then forced the air crew to take off with him, three parachutes, and $200,000 in extortion money. But, hey—that ole D. B. was somethin' (we can almost see the regulars on their barstools nodding their heads).

An old German saying is appropriate: "It doesn't follow the rules, but it's cunning and successful." Similarly, this sentiment probably prevailed at the Wittenberg bars ("A monk from *here*, out of *our* city!"), since his heretic hearing in Augsburg and his defense in front of the (in)famous Johann Eck in Leipzig had made himself famous. What *exactly* the details were about—whether people understood or even shared Luther's theological criticisms, demands, and suggested reforms for the church—hasn't played much of a role to counter the "homeboy" Luther myths since December 10, 1520.

What we do know about that crucial date is this: a fire was kindled in front of the Elster gate in Wittenberg. Martin Luther, Philip Melanchthon, and some students threw a papal bull excommunicating Luther into the fire. The papal proclamation had summoned Luther to recant his Ninety-Five Theses within sixty days, otherwise he would be outlawed (and pursued via the papal version of wanted posters). The chief papal negotiator, Johann Eck, had brought with him the official notification from Rome to the public disputation in Leipzig in June 1519. Did Luther cave in to the threat? No, he burned it publicly (ain't he somethin'!).

The pope's reaction came promptly: on January 3, 1521, Pope Leo X signed the official bull of excommunication, the notarized document of exclusion from the church and the revocation of any legal rights of due process. It said:

> Now because Martinus has not recanted his fallacies within the
> set period, thus he has officially become a heretic and is to be
> viewed as such, and all of Christ's faithful should flee from him

or shun him. And all who follow him, protect him, feed him, care for him, or embolden themselves in any way to assist and give him advice, help, and abetment have no concerns—they will be viewed as banned and cursed people, they and their descendants, who with that forfeit all honor, dignity, and possessions.[2]

From now on it was dangerous to have any contact with Luther at all. The level of public excitement was ratcheting up a notch (today we would say "the media hype was in full swing"). But Emperor Charles V didn't send a hit man to Wittenberg but sent instead an invitation to yet another diet in the imperial city of Worms (yet another tedious imperial affair!). Come again? "To our dear, honorable, reverend doctor Martinus Luther," he wrote on March 26, 1521. That's how one writes to a man the pope has just outlawed and asked people to kill on sight?

"I don't want to reap glory and honor with my books and pamphlets. . . . I certainly don't act out of greed for honor, possessions, or acclaim!"

The ruling city officials in Wittenberg didn't let themselves be intimidated by the ban: Luther and his three companions had a very modern (for the times) "rolling cart" made available to them, an open wagon with three horses, as well as an allowance and a mounted herald as a bodyguard, whose flag with the imperial eagle—easy to recognize from a distance—would effectively warn away highwaymen or robber barons.

As Luther neared the city of Erfurt on his way to Worms (on Saturday, April 6, 1521), forty horsemen approached him: the university rector Johann Crotus and his students invited Luther to a dinner reception at the Augustinian monastery where Luther formerly lived. The streets were lined with jubilant crowds, and at the end of the triumphal procession

---

2. Bernhard, *Martin Luther Hausbuch*, 568.

awaited Luther's old friend Johann Lang. Someone asked the reformer to hold the service for Low Sunday.[3] The church was packed to the walls. Similar spectacles occurred in other cities along the route. Now Luther could no longer deny it: he was being celebrated as a hero of the people. Against his will? Or was it also a little self-orchestrated?

"I don't want to reap glory and honor with my books and pamphlets. Almost everyone denounces my vehemence. But I think what is being dealt with in our time will, with peace, soon be forgotten without one noticing. Who can say whether or not the spirit with its impetuosity propels me since I certainly don't act out of greed for honor, possessions, or acclaim!"[4]

Just how Luther's entry into the city of Worms on the morning of April 16, 1521, was received (when he "hit the street," so to speak), we know from the meticulous notes of a Roman informant, the papal nuncio Girolamo Aleandro:

> From the hasty running of the people, I gathered that the great supreme heretic had entered. I myself sent one of my people out who reported back to me that up to a hundred mercenaries on horseback had escorted him all the way to the city gate. With three comrades sitting in a wagon, he moved into the city, surrounded by eight horsemen, and took his lodging near the Saxon princes. As he stepped out of the wagon, his demonic eyes looked around and he said: "God will be with me!" Then he came into a parlor where he ate with ten of the twelve men. After the meal, everyone walked there in order to see him. An awestruck priest touched Luther's garb reverently three times as if he had held a relic in his hands. Soon, it will mean he can perform miracles.[5]

Just in case Luther couldn't actually perform miracles himself (he couldn't), there were already miraculous amulets, small medallions, and

---

3. For those not familiar with the liturgical calendar, Low Sunday is the Sunday after Easter, named in contrast to the "high" day of Easter Sunday.

4. Bernhard, *Martin Luther Hausbuch*, 22–23.

5. Saager, *Luther-Anekdoten*, 92–93.

images of Martin Luther for sale on the market tables in Worms. "Nothing else is being bought more, even in the court of the emperor, than pictures of Luther! They were so quickly offered for sale and sold out that I could not get one anymore," a papal representative complained.[6] What a bummer (and odd that he also wanted one—purely out of professional interest, I'm sure).

Did Luther enjoy the star hype?

We don't know. Did he find his popularity to be a protective shield since one could not simply kill a famous hero of the people? Rather unlikely. Today even dictators must pay attention to their international reputation or risk being unseated. Emperor Charles V, the pope, and the German bishops, however, could have cared less about public opinion, though they could never afford to ignore the sentiments of the local rulers and power brokers. The elites were, ironically, dependent on the not-so-elites for their power (and money). In this respect, it was important for Luther's survival that he have a "good name" with *those* rulers. This he obtained not through staged vanity but by simple courage—and through an authentic, sometimes annoying, and thoroughly sincere childlike piety.

We can rightly ask why the Saxon Prince Frederick the Wise so often, so discretely, and so successfully kept his protecting hand on Luther. Did he only use him as a convenient instrument for political pinpricks against the emperor and pope? Or was the whole conflict a bit of a royal pain, so that he instructed his chief diplomat, George Spalatin, to keep on top of it, as we would say today? Or was Frederick the Wise actually taken by Luther's charisma and protected him out of personal conviction? Whatever the case, the University of Wittenberg was the most visited in Germany since Luther and Melanchthon had begun teaching there.

"I rode to the lodging house of Prince Frederick," Luther shared later regarding his arrival in Worms, "but he felt uneasy for my safety since I had now come to the imperial diet."[7] Did Luther meet with him personally? Or was Luther denied an audience so the cagey Frederick could avoid

---

6.   Landgraf, *Martin Luther*, 164.
7.   Mayer, *Martin Luther*, 92.

being labeled a friend of the heretic before the case was decided? In the 2003 movie *Luther*, Luther (Joseph Fiennes) and Frederick the Wise (Sir Peter Ustinov) encounter one another in person. Whether that was ever the case remained Luther and Frederick's secret.

Did Luther just trigger the Reformation?

What was perhaps the most momentous political, intellectual, and spiritual upheaval in German history happened neither by calculation nor by chance. Rather, it came about because, in some undefinable sense, the time was ripe. Because a potential reaction had long been searching for a catalyst. Because something inchoate was rumbling subtly below the surface of the times and needed a flash point, a triggering agent for the "something" to crystalize.

Let's look briefly at Luther from the perspective of modern-day "star hype." Someone becomes a celebrity (something beyond just being successful) when he or she functions as a screen onto which we, their humble admirers, can project a *desired* life. When someone can do something that I cannot do but enjoy greatly (Lebron James shooting a game-winning three-pointer at the buzzer, for example), I elevate him in my thinking. Or when someone simply does something I would never dare to attempt (like astronaut Scott Kelly being blasted into space aboard a rocket built by the lowest bidder). Or when a person changes the world with an idea that I would never think of in a million years (say, Mark Zuckerberg and Facebook). When someone is able to distill into words what millions of people also want to say but could never express themselves. Such crystallization points, such public figures that encapsulate the longings and wishes of millions of people—we admire them, we listen to them, and we adore them. They are the stars to which we lift our adoring and obedient gazes.

Martin Luther was such a figure five hundred years ago. But is he also that in the twenty-first century?

One can hardly identify anymore with his fears and worries ("How do I find a merciful God?"). Nor is one afraid of being burned at the stake nowadays (outside of ISIL-occupied Syria at least). Luther's hopes and wishes ("that everyone has the Holy Scriptures and may read them") are more than fulfilled. There are at least 636 versions of the complete Bible in various world languages, and some 3,223 New Testaments and portions of the Bible in translation.[8] His opponents ("the antichrist on the throne of St. Peter," as Luther referred to the pope) have come around as well. Just as the pope was himself something of a media star and a darling of the public in Luther's day, so also today's pope has toured the world with great acclaim, but with a dramatically different message. Pope Francis recently reflected that, "We cannot serve God well if we hunger after power and wealth."[9] So take that, Pope Leo.

What is there then to celebrate?

Luther's impact, for one, which released an explosion of the mind whose shockwaves are still perceptible even today in religion, philosophy, politics, culture, and society. There is also a name to celebrate, which Luther himself made possible: Evangelical Christians (from the Greek word *euangelion*, the "good news" or gospel). It was Luther who started the recovery of the gospel of God's grace for every person.

And speaking of names: Margarete Luther named her child Martin because November 10 (his birthday) was the day before the feast day of Saint Martin.[10] There was no birth certificate or entry in the baptismal register. When Martin matriculated at the university to study law in Erfurt in April 1501, the entry in the university directory read, "Martinus Ludher ex Mansfelt" ("Martin Luther from Mansfelt"). It is the oldest remaining document containing his name.

8. "Scripture and Language Statistics 2016," Wycliffe Global Alliance.
9. Francis I, "Be On Guard."
10. His feast is associated with the coming of winter ("St. Martin comes riding on a white horse" was a common statement), the celebration of the fall harvest, and the slaughter of meat with feasting and bonfires ("His Martinmas will come as it does to every hog"), and his revered cloak (his *cappa* in Latin) gave us our English words *chapel* and *chaplain*.

Chapter 18

Luther Named His Supporters "Protestants"

Seven princes and fourteen cities protested on March 1529 that their faith should be voted on. These—and initially only these—were named "Protestants." So, no, it didn't come from Luther.

How did it come about?

After the Diet in Worms in 1521, Emperor Charles V excommunicated Luther and banned his teachings (this is the so-called Edict of Worms). Rather stupidly, he postdated the document, as if it had been the decision of all the members of the imperial diet (see chapter 9, "Luther Sometimes Played Tricks and Told Lies"). Several princes fought back against this later misattribution. How? By simply ignoring the imperial ban against Luther. And for the princes it was also a lot cheaper not to send their law enforcement agencies out to apprehend the heretic. When people refrain from doing something long enough (like, in those days, enforcing an imperial ban), it was eventually accepted as normal. In 1526, again at a diet, this time in Speyer, the emperor *legalized* the non-persecution of the "new believers." Each prince would be allowed to keep their confession of faith in their respective territories as they considered right. The staunchly Catholic Charles conceded with a heavy heart.

Ostensibly, it only meant this: the diet passed the law. Subtly, however, it was also the rending of the confessional unity of the empire. Although no one had stated this intent, the result was that the empire began to split into "old Catholic" and "new Lutheran" regions. That also led to social implications.

If the Luther ban was brutally enforced in one principality, the persecuted Luther sympathizers escaped to a more tolerant neighboring kingdom. Some of those who left, however, had built the economic success of their homelands and formed the intellectual elite (the upper crust, as we'd say today). Did this mean that only the more backwards folk remained behind? Orthodox, but dumb and poor?

Emperor Charles V, for one, was worried. So worried that he extended an invitation for a second diet in Speyer. Once again he himself was unfortunately hindered from attending—a pesky war against France, very time-consuming, sorry—and once again he sent his brother Ferdinand. The brother allowed, without further ado, a vote on April 19, 1529, to repeal the imperial recess. A sort of legal click on the "delete" button. The emperor's representative pleaded with those present, speaking somewhat contradictorily that while the emperor had been correct three years ago, it could now be seen that he was mistaken. Ergo, vote yes to say no!

Who was now in favor of declaring religious tolerance a crazy idea? The majority! In the wake of the vote, Elector Johann of Saxony, Landgrave Philip I of Hesse, Margrave George of Brandenburg-Ansbach, the dukes Ernest I and Francis of Brunswick-Lüneburg, Prince Wolfgang of Anhalt-Köthen, and Count Wilhelm of Fürstenberg, along with their chancellors, advisers, and court chaplains (as well as Luther's close friend and fellow Bible translator Philip Melanchthon), all stood up and . . . walked out! Left the hall. They simply refused to accept the election results.

Outside, Gregor von Brück wrote a "protestation" on behalf of the entourage of the Saxon princes, in which it was expounded (in a somewhat convoluted and mixed-up way) that they would "repeal the repeal" of the imperial recess on grounds of conscience, regardless of what the majority decided. And not to be outdone, the mayors of the imperial cities also protested.

They wanted to present their protestation to the imperial representative, Ferdinand, but he refused to accept it. In this respect, he "protested" as well. Not until almost a week later, on April 25, was a protest document summarizing the position of the evangelical cities and princes (henceforth named the *Instrumentum Appelationis* or "Instrument of Appeal") delivered to him. From here—and not from Luther—comes the word *Protestant*.

Chapter 19

Luther Invented German Proverbs

Not all of them, of course, but many—some of which we also use in English.

Hochmut kommt vor dem Fall—Pride goes before the fall.

Der Mensch lebt nicht vom Brot allein—Man does not live by bread alone.

Aus dem Herzen keine Mördergrube machen—Don't make a den of thieves from the heart; or, speak frankly.

Was du nicht willst, dass man dir tu, das füg auch keinem anderen zu—Do unto others as you would want them to do unto you.

Wer den Schaden hat, braucht für den Spott nicht zu sorgen—One should not mock the afflicted.

Kleine Kinder, kleine Sorgen. Große Kinder, große Sorgen—Little children, little worries. Big children, big worries.

Wer den Pfennig nicht ehrt, ist des Talers nicht wert—A penny saved is a penny earned.

Ist es dem Esel zu wohl, geht er aufs Eis—If the donkey is doing too well, he might go out on the thin ice; or, pride goes before a fall.

Then, there are thousands of colloquial idioms, such as:

Dich sticht doch der Hafer—You're feeling your oats.

Dir juckt das Fell—That itches your skin.

Du musst in den sauren Apfel beißen—You have to swallow the bitter pill.

Lass dich nicht an der Nase herumführen—Don't be led around by the nose.

Will mir nicht das Maul verbrennen—I don't want to burn my mouth; or, better to say nothing than to say anything at all.

All from Luther, or what? Not exactly.

A figure of speech (such as the donkey and ice above) becomes "proverbial" only when a great many people use it very often and it becomes embedded in the language and culture. Finding "fitting formulations" has less to do with ingenuity than it does with attentive listening. That is what Martin Luther could obviously do very well. His explanation for how he went about translating the Bible became famous: "One doesn't have to ask the letter of the Latin language how one should speak German; rather one must ask the mom at home, the children in the yard, and the simple man, and see the same in their mouths, how they talk, and then translate so they understand it."[1] This sentence itself created an idiom that is popular even today in Germany: "Look at the crowd's mouth."

Should we conclude that Luther snuck in existing and conventional idioms into his translation of the Bible? Yes, insofar as they accurately reproduced the meaning of the original Hebrew or Greek texts.

Martin, a son of a miner, finished his bachelor's degree at nineteen years old, his master's in general humanities at twenty-two at the University of Erfurt, and at twenty-six a bachelor's degree in Bible and linguistics at the University of Wittenberg. At thirty he became a professor and succeeded the honorable professor Johann von Staupitz. However, instead of showing off his exceptionally high level of education or retreating to the ivory tower of scholarship with a small, noble circle of scholars, Luther searched . . . the public streets and alleyways, so to say.

---

1. Friedenthal, *Luther*, 373.

"When I come to the pulpit, I thus intend only to preach to the servants and maids. For Doctor Jonas's or Melanchthon's sake, I would not appear [in the pulpit] one single time. They can surely read it in the Scripture. When one, however, wants only to preach to the highly educated and teachers and speak masterpieces, the poor people stand there like a cow."[2]

To instruct only these "dumb cow" people, however, didn't hold water among the intellectuals in the hierarchical society of Luther's day that clearly marked out one's social status. But Luther had learned something from these bovine folk beforehand—namely, how to speak clearly at their level. "Never before had a professor so thoroughly renounced the educated nobility like Luther. That he had remained inwardly a man of the people despite school, university, monastery, and lectern made him into a hero of the people."[3]

When one looks at the 350 printed materials of Luther, the song lyrics, the adaptations, the animal fables of the poet Aesop, the sermons, the 2,585 personal and legal letters, and the roughly seven thousand table talks (never mind the many sources he could have "borrowed" from linguistically)—one can identify these elements: the classical Greek and Roman poets, the Hebrew and Greek Bibles, the church fathers of the first three centuries after Christ, and the many expressions which he had heard and which he wrote down in his private notebook. Four hundred and eighty-nine maxims, bon mots, aphorisms, rhymes, and figures of speech were collected by Martin Luther. His own personal "treasure chest" of words, so to speak.

For the common people, it didn't really matter when they listened to his sermons if this or that memorable phrase was invented by the reformer or only found elsewhere or was a modified quote by Vergil, Seneca, Solomon, David, Paul, or Augustine. For the world at large—and understandably so in the oral transmission of the last five centuries of history—everything

2. Schilling, *Luther zum Vergnügen*, 25.
3. Reiners, *Stilkunst*, 192.

somehow became "Luther words." Above all, when one wanted to garnish a word of advice, it was stronger coming with Luther's authority. Consider the iterations of his reminder to the young to learn diligently:

Was Hänschen nicht lernt, lernt Hans nimmermehr—What little Hans didn't learn, Hans will never learn. (Somewhat like our saying, "You can't teach an old dog new tricks.")

This idea was then also positively expressed:

Früh übt sich, wer ein Meister werden will—Those who want to become a master practice early.

These were modifications (and simplifications) of the older original:

Früh krümmt sich, was ein Haken werden will—That which wants to become a hook bends early.

However, the idea that Martin Luther was unconsciously describing his own early signs of rebelliousness is rather improbable.

"*Wer anderen eine Grube gräbt, fällt selbst hinein*" ("The one who digs a hole for another falls into it oneself") goes back further still to Solomon's book of Proverbs (26:27).

"It is easier for a camel to go through the eye of a needle than for someone who is rich to enter the kingdom of God" is a direct quote from Jesus in Matthew 19:24. Modified but still in Luther's German Bible to this day are expressions like "*das eine tun, das andere nicht lassen*" ("do that, but allow the other," Matt. 23:23), "*perlen vor die Säue werfen*" ("to throw pearls before swine," Matt. 7:6), "*nicht mehr wissen, wo rechts und links ist*" ("do not know anymore where right and left are," Jonah 4:11), and "*die Haare zu Berge stehen*" ("hair stands on end," Job 4:15).

Can one conclude that Luther created many common expressions still used today in his translation of the Bible? Yes, he did. At any rate, more than Shakespeare ("To be or not to be"), Goethe ("So this, then, was the kernel of the brute!"), or the fairy tales of the Brothers Grimm ("And if they didn't die . . ."—or as we have anglicized it: "And they all lived happily ever after").

As Jacob and Wilhelm Grimm wrote their sixteen-volume German dictionary in 1838, they praised "the noble, almost marvelous purity" of Luther's language. Equally romantics and critical scholars, they went head over heels with downright exaltation of Luther: "How Luther reached the language in which he translated the Bible is to this very hour for me unfathomable. This written language gives our politically and religiously carved-up Germany a literary unity. In the Bible Luther's language is captivated by the awe of the omnipresent Spirit of God, always with a certain dignity. In his polemic pamphlets he turned to a rawness, which was just as repugnant as it was magnificent. The same man who could swear like a fishwife[4] could also be soft like a gentle virgin. Wild like a storm, which uproots oak trees; soft like a southwest breeze, which caresses violets."[5]

I think their sense of Luther is true. Consequently, however, his opponents singled out the especially crass sayings for contempt while his admirers assumed an attitude of veneration for all that was elegant in his works. Certainly Luther had both extremes.

"Tell him he can lick my butt" does *not* come from Luther, but rather from the German author and poet Johann Wolfgang von Goethe. It appears in the third act of his 1774 play *Götz von Berlichingen*. The play takes its name from an imperial knight, Gottfried "Götz" von Berlichigen (1480–1562), also known as Götz of the Iron Hand, who was a mercenary and poet and a contemporary of Luther (1483–1546). He had fought in the German Peasants' War in 1525 on the side of the rebels, and whether or not he ever said that can't be proven. But from what we know from Luther, it is indicative of the times.

This issue of false attribution is perhaps easier to understand when we

---

4. The wives (or daughters) of fishermen, who sold fish in the market and offset the perishable nature of their wares with aggressive and often foul sales pitches.
5. Wolf, *Luther*, 285.

consider this example: Johann Kinau, author of the book *Seefahrt ist not!* (*Seafaring Is a Must!*), wrote, "And even if I sink to the bottom of the sea, I sink then forever only into God's hand." (On May 16, 1916, during the Battle of Jutland in World War I, that became the sad reality for Johann Kinau.)

A hundred years later theologian and ambassador for the Reformation Jubilee 2017 Margot Käßmann stepped down from her positions as council president of the Evangelical Church in Germany and bishop of Hanover, and quoted this sentence as her "religious conviction and experience from past crises": "You cannot fall more deeply than in the hand of God."[6]

And those clever reporters at the press conference probably nodded to themselves and made a mental note: "Bible." "Likely from Luther." But it is not Luther at all. Nor is it from the unfortunate sailor Johann Kinau. It is a song lyric from the German poet Arno Pötzsch (1900–1956).

So this business of proper attribution is tricky, to say the least. The number of comforting, wise, or pious proverbs, sayings, or figures of speech that aren't from Luther but are ascribed to him for the sake of simplicity may actually increase in the future. Because of the Reformation Jubilee. Or because of television shows. Or movie theaters. Who knows? "Life is like a box of chocolates," perhaps?

---

6. "Musste Margot Käßmann unbedingt zurücktreten?" *Die Welt.*

Chapter 20

Luther Nailed Ninety-Five Theses to the Wittenberg Church Door

Probably not. I'm sure this will be a huge disappointment to Luther fans. There never were the "hammer blows under which the medieval Catholic Church cracked." Although for 450 years, millions of school children, confirmands, and theology and history students were told so by their parents, clergy, teachers, and university lecturers. Sometimes with emotion and a trembling voice. On a "windy Saturday" before All Saints' Day, the professor walked with "thoughtful steps the fifteen minutes from the Black Monastery to the palace church" to strike there a poster of theses (debate topics) in Latin on the northern entrance door with a hammer, "single-handedly, audibly, and visibly during the midday ringing of the bells."[1] Great drama, but all legend.

What should we think, then, of the amusing Luther-double who stands today at the door of the palace church in Wittenberg? If the Roman Catholic world didn't collapse, then neither should the touristic world, truth be told. But how could we so heavily disappoint the millions of Chinese, Japanese, Indian, and American tourists? (Much less deny Wittenberg their commercial tax from the visitors!)

---

1. Wolf, *Luther*, 235.

Now let's just slowly recount the sequence of events: From where does this story with the hammer actually originate?

"Luther, burning with zeal for true piety, released his theses on indulgences. He posted these publicly near the Wittenberg palace the day before All Saints' Day in 1517,"[2] Philip Melanchthon wrote. A close lifelong friend of Luther, professor of Greek at the University of Wittenberg, ally of the Reformation, important fellow translator, editor, and proofreader of Martin Luther's Bible translation, Melanchthon was a key witness. Except: he wrote this long after Luther's death in 1546 in the preface to the second volume of the collected works of his friend, by which time Luther's historical halo already vibrantly shone.

Why should it not be the case?

First: during the time of the alleged hammering of the theses, the then twenty-year-old Melanchthon was still busy at the University of Tübingen. In his memories around forty years later, he sometimes erred. To provide a couple of examples, Luther supposedly taught physics, and indulgence preacher Johann Tetzel supposedly publicly burned Luther's theses. Neither is true, of course.

Second: there is no single eyewitness account for the "audible, visible, and public" hammering of the theses, although Luther's enemies would have possibly earned informant fees for such information and may have made an impression on the bishops and princes.

Third: on September 4, 1517, Martin Luther had already written a set of theses. Exactly one hundred. One hundred "short, sharply formulated sentences" *against* the predominant Scholastic theology of the medieval philosopher Thomas Aquinas (1225–1274) and Anselm of Canterbury (1033–1109). Luther wanted his theses to be discussed by his students in Wittenberg as an exam topic, and then he would present the results at a conference of the European order of St. Augustine at the University of Heidelberg in April 1518. For such "disputations" there was a well-oiled and efficient operating channel: the professor submitted the paper to the dean of the university. He would approve or change it. Then the paper

---

2. Prause, *Niemand hat Kolumbus ausgelacht*, 81.

would be printed and distributed to the students. If the theses were supposed to be *publicly* discussed, the caretaker and envoy of the university
tacked the paper on all (!) of the church doors in Wittenberg. With the
date, time, and place of the planned event.

This is how it happened with the Scholastic critique in September.
Why did Luther supposedly abandon this correct and consensual official channel six weeks later with his critique of indulgences? It would
have made little sense to go *around* the university dean to nail ninety-five
formulated theses in Latin only on one church door for illiterate people
passing by and thus risk a spat with his employer. Not to mention that
absolutely no concrete discussion meeting was scheduled that one could
be publicly invited to on the bulletin board.

Fourth: when Luther's former colleague Christoph von Scheurl complained four months later at the beginning of March 1518 about why he
received the theses much later, Luther responded to him, "It was neither my
plan nor my intention to publicize them greatly. On the contrary, I wanted
to exchange views first of all only with a few here."[3] Would someone write
that who had also pasted revolutionary, illegal posters? The most substantial argument against the hammering of the theses is Luther himself.

Fifth: from June 1525 onward, he and his wife Katharina ran a large
and very populated guesthouse, and the sayings of a rather more talk-
ative and pleasantly reminiscent Martin Luther were documented in the
written notes of countless conversational partners. Every spectacular joke,
every adventurous situation, every dangerous, tragic, or weird scene of
his life—yes, even the most intimate or embarrassing moments—was at
some point related by Luther. In none of the seven thousand table talks,
eight hundred publications from his pen, 2,585 letters, or countless sermons does he mention once that he single-handedly nailed a placard onto
the palace church door! In detailing all his other public victories and
defeats—the interrogation by Cardinal Thomas Cajetan at the Diet of
Augsburg in 1518, the appearance in front of Emperor Charles V at the

---

3. Mayer, *Martin Luther*, 61.

Diet of Worms in 1521, his secret hermitage in the Wartburg castle and the Coburg Fortress—not one table talk or letter references this. Concerning a hammering of theses on October 31, 1517, there was not a single question from anyone. Why should Luther have concealed this detail of what was already recognized in his lifetime as his most far-reaching feat?

As soon as two Luther scholars, Erwin Iserloh and Heinrich Steitz, posed these questions in 1961, it provoked a fervent discussion among historians, which by 2015 yielded approximately three hundred scholarly essays and articles. All the more since 2006 when a notation from the estate of the overworked assistant and traveling companion Georg Rörer (1492–1557) emerged to the effect that the theses would have hung on the church doors on October 31, 1517. Whether nailed, pasted, or tacked there by Luther himself, the university caretaker, or the students, Rörer's note is older than the one from Melanchthon and therefore considered "more substantial." Really?

Rörer's ordination to the office of deacon on May 14, 1525, in the Wittenberg palace church was truly the first evangelical ordination in the world. Rörer's writings on the table talks, sermons, and presentations of Martin Luther, Philip Melanchthon, and Johannes Bugenhagen were collected in 1539 in the four volumes of the first Wittenberg edition of Luther's German works—but because of his unauthorized corrections of Luther's texts and his depictions of the events, he had to give up his pastoral office in 1537 and even leave Wittenberg in 1551. Even if his note had been accurate, *hammer blows* don't resound throughout Wittenberg. For understandable reasons, this information hasn't been so willingly published. The tourism, as you well know . . .

What really happened then on Reformation Day?

Luther was appalled by the popular rule of thumb: "Donate something for St. Peter's Basilica and show the receipt to the good God. Then you need neither to regret, nor confess, nor do penance, nor ask for forgiveness." By whose order did the demagogue Johann Tetzel shout this malarkey all over the market squares? By order of the pope. Who were his jointly responsible representatives in the region? Bishop Jerome Schulz of

Brandenburg and Archbishop Albert von Mainz-Magdeburg. Luther sent his Ninety-Five Theses *to these two*. In them it says, among other things, "that Christians set out to do everything to follow Christ, their master, through pain, death, and anguish. They are supposed to confide in him so that they will come through all temptation and affliction to eternal life, not by thinking that they own it in peaceful carelessness."[4] With the theses, he attached an accompanying letter.

"Donate something for St. Peter's Basilica and show the receipt to the good God. Then you need neither to regret, nor confess, nor do penance, nor ask for forgiveness."
—popular view of indulgences

The tone of the letter's introduction, typical of the time, makes clear how outrageous it was to criticize a bishop: "Forgive me most reverend father in Christ, most serene prince, that I, human dust, own such a degree of presumptuousness and dare to even think of a letter to your noble highness! Jesus, the Lord, is my witness that I—well aware of my lowness and wretchedness—have long delayed what I now carry out in an improper way. May your highness hence be so merciful as to graciously accept my plea for your episcopal leniency."[5] Only after all this follows the summary of the Ninety-Five Theses studded with Scripture passages.

Without the traces of smarminess above, Luther sent his theses to a third recipient: his friend Johann Lang. That was it, however. Luther hoped to stimulate an epistolary discussion among theologians and later perhaps a public session. But it didn't happen. Not even among Luther's university colleagues in Wittenberg, much less the wide world. "I wrote two letters with the request to prohibit the shameless activities and

4. Ibid.
5. Dithmar, *Durch Gottes Gnade bin ich wohlauf,* 14.

blasphemous speech of the indulgence preachers. But no one gave the pathetic monk any attention at all."[6]

What was the reaction? What happened next?

Nothing happened, absolutely nothing. In the monastery in Erfurt, his friend Lang read the theses fourteen days later, but in Wittenberg? Six weeks went by, no response. Only foggy November serenity on the bank of the Elbe River. (Wouldn't there have been something after a dramatic "hammer action" on the church doors?) However, to dismiss Luther's documents from October 31, 1517, was the most serious management mistake Archbishop Albert and Bishop Jerome Schulz ever committed. Perhaps one of the most serious in European history: at the end of December 1517, Luther's Wittenberg friends printed the Ninety-Five Theses on leaflets, distributed them, and "in nearly fourteen days the same flowed throughout all of Germany because all the world complained about the indulgences, especially Tetzel's article,"[7] as Luther himself said.

A minister living at that time named Friedrich Myconius estimated that the dissemination took a little longer, but nevertheless marveled: "In four weeks, the theses had passed through almost all of Christendom as if the angels were running the news about."[8]

Who was the first to react?

Johann Tetzel, who else! In January 1518, he complained about the cheeky monk-lecturer from Wittenberg in 109 polemically formulated theses that were typical of Tetzel. He sent three hundred printed copies to Wittenberg. Although the good Professor Martin was against it, Luther's students publicly burned the Tetzel papers and "afterward extinguished the flames with plenty of beer."[9] Perhaps this is where the German idiom "to cool one's courageous little nerves" comes from, which basically means to sedate them in beer!

Luther replied with a pamphlet titled "Sermon on Indulgences and

6. Prause, *Niemand hat Kolumbus ausgelacht*, 88.
7. Saager, *Luther-Anekdoten*, 65.
8. Ibid.
9. Wolf, *Thesen*, 127.

Grace." But first he traveled to Heidelberg in April 1518 to a conference of the Order of St. Augustine and realized on his return that the matter had escalated: indulgence preacher (and ex-grand inquisitor of Poland) Johann Tetzel had upped the ante by fifty more theses, delivered them by courier to Luther's residence in Wittenberg in June 1518, and threatened him with a legal Inquisition prosecution. When Luther received the official invitation on August 7, 1518, to come to Rome to be interrogated there as a suspected heretic, it was clear to everyone: *the pope* had the Ninety-Five Theses on his desk!

The battle had begun.

Chapter 21

Luther Threw an Inkhorn at the Devil

Probably not. Luther had a melancholic—if not quite depressive—side, which especially came to light in the winter of 1521–22 when he hid under a false name in the Wartburg castle near Eisenach.

Tired of solitude, heavily doubting himself and his work, worried terribly about good friends who were under determined and powerful enemies—Luther, completely in line with the thought and atmosphere of his culture, felt that everything was a personal attack of a very real, living Satan. Luther shared candidly his perception that a poltergeist was robbing him of sleep (he claimed it also disturbed the sleep of one of the castle's female guests; see chapter 1, "Luther Was a Superstitious Person"). But he never claimed that he looked to an inkhorn that same night to get some peace and quiet. Not to mention that ink was expensive and Luther needed a lot of it while he was translating the New Testament!

The historical heart of this legend may be: Luther spoke once of being amazed by the effect that his Ninety-Five Theses and his first essay had triggered not only in the people but also in scholars, artists, princes, the emperor, and the pope. He had, metaphorically speaking, "cast out the devil with ink." True. But what came of it when successive readers couldn't distinguish between the literal and the figurative meaning of a verbal image? The following.

From 1650 onward there were paintings of Luther in the study of the Wartburg that showed a blue spot on the wall! Needless to say, many visitors searched earnestly for it—behind the green stove or slanting over the heavy writing desk—and the operators of the Wartburg castle were already business-minded enough to care about such a speck! One should not disappoint guests, after all. In the centuries without video surveillance, however, it was inevitable that shameless visitors scratched off a little paint from this spot. As a Luther relic so to speak, as a strangely appropriate souvenir. That's why on the one hand the exorcistic ink splash had to be recreated a zillion times, and why on the other hand there is a hole in the plaster today. A dent painted over cleanly with the wall color. Despite this, the current chief press officer of the Wartburg, Andreas Vokert, says that there are now and again visitors who wanted to see the devil's ink stain.

Tongue-in-cheek, the eloquent satirical poet Heinrich Heine (1797–1856) correctly understood Luther's inkhorn toss in his nineteenth-century poem, "Germany, a Winter Tale." He knew that freedom of the press is always dangerous for dictators. His writings were forbidden by censors, so he had to flee to Paris. He said, "When Luther translated the New Testament, he became so troubled by the devil that he threw an inkhorn at his head. Since then the devil has had such a great shyness of ink and printer's ink!"[1]

---

1. Heine, *Sämtliche Werke*, 16.

Chapter 22

Luther's Last Words Were, "We Are Beggars, That Is True."

Well, he didn't *say* it. His friend Justus Jonas found a note in his bedroom directly after Luther's last breath, on which was written, "*Wir seyn pettler hoc est verum*"—"We are beggars, that is true."

When Luther actually wrote this note, however, no one knows. The quote was also not new. When the Old Testament was (finally) presented in German, Luther spoke of the distance between his own life experiences and those of the biblical figures: "No one who hasn't been a shepherd or a farmer for five years can understand [the Roman poet] Virgil. No one understands the letters of [the Roman politician] Cicero who hasn't been active in a great political system for twenty years. And no one should believe they have sufficiently tasted the Holy Scripture when they haven't led the church for one hundred years with the prophets. *We* [in comparison to them] are beggars, that is true!"[1]

Or had Luther written the note during mediation talks between Count Gebhard I von Mansfeld-Vorderort and his brother Albrecht VII, who were arguing over their inheritance and asked Luther to join them as mediator? On January 23, 1546, he—yet again—left Wittenberg for

---

1. Schilling, *Luther zum Vergnügen*, 103.

his hometown, Eisleben. Because of floodwaters he could not cross the Saale River, and upon continuing the journey suffered a heart attack in Rißdorf. On February 14, he had to stop his sermon at St. Andreas's Church in Eisleben ("I am too weak. We want to leave it at that").[2] On February 16, he made yet another macabre joke at the table: "When I come back home again to Wittenberg, I want to lay myself in the casket and give the maggots a plump doctor to eat![3]

On the morning of February 17, after at least a three-week tussle, "the peevish quarrel" of Gebhard and Albrecht was finally settled in court. "But I became sore and anxious in the chest like never before, a compression of the heart as if I was suffocating,"[4] Luther complained in the afternoon.

Angina pectoris instead of joy over the peaceable agreement? Possibly apprehensive, his sons Johannes, Martin, and Paul came to the upper floor of the house. They were nineteen, fourteen, and twelve years old and lived with Martin's brother Jacob, not far from there. Count Albrecht von Mansfeld and his wife tried to infuse the dying man with "unicorn," a supposedly curative drink made from crushed cetacean teeth and wine. The town clerk and notary for the count, Johann Albrecht and his wife, in whose house Luther lived during the negotiations, looked after him. His friend Johannes Aurifaber and his servant Ambrosius, court chaplain Michael Caelius, and friend and fellow reformer Justus Jonas immediately sent for two doctors from Eisleben. They all stood in the late evening of February 17 around Luther's bed. None of these thirteen witnesses, however, heard "We are beggars, that is true."

What they did hear was later transmitted divergently. *Table Talks* cowriter Johannes Aurifaber said the dying Luther prayed:

Almighty, eternal, merciful Lord and God, who is a father of our dear Lord Jesus Christ, I know for certain that you can and

---

2. Wolf, *Thüringer Porträts*, 632.
3. Neumann, *Luthers Leiden*, 144.
4. Fassmann, *Die Großen der Weltgeschichte*, 144.

also want to uphold everything that you said because you cannot lie: your word is true. You promised me at the beginning your only beloved son Jesus Christ; the same came and delivered me from the Devil, death, hell, and sin. Afterward you gave me, for my great assurance through your gracious will, the sacraments of holy baptism and Communion, through which the forgiveness of sins, eternal life, and all heavenly things were offered to me. On such, your offering, I have used the same and in faith I have trusted firmly in your word and have received it. Therefore, I don't now doubt that I am satisfied and saved from the Devil, death, hell, and sin. This is my hour and your divine will, so with peace and joy I want to happily depart to your Word, amen.[5]

That is certainly moving. But also, amazingly, a lot of words for a deathly sick man who three days earlier had to stop preaching. Does a dying, "suffocating" man talk like that? Sounds more like a well-thought-out theological bequest, a confession of faith, which summarizes all the important points of evangelical theology. One may safely suppose it's more Aurifaber than Luther.

"Into your hand I entrust my spirit.
You have delivered me, faithful God."

Or did Count Albrecht understand the whispers correctly? "Dear God, it hurts and I'm afraid. I'm coming! Take my little soul to you!"[6]

Justus Jonas, who accompanied him over the ice-flooded meadows of the Saale River, reported, "He said three times, '*In manus tuas commendo spiritum meum, redimisti me, Deu veritatis*'" ("Into your hand I entrust my spirit. You have delivered me, faithful God."). A verse from Psalm 31,

5. Aland, *Luther deutsch*, 289.
6. Dieckmann, "Martini Himmelfahrt."

which Jesus prayed on the cross. For a lifelong Latin-quoting Bible translator, a very likely last word, in my opinion.

However, Luther's ultimate last word was attested consistently by those present. Around eleven at night, Luther was already drifting away. Justus Jonas shouted at him (others remember Michael Caelius doing the shouting to the hard-of-hearing reformer), "Revered, beloved father, now dying, do you want to confess to your Lord Jesus Christ, our savior and redeemer, as well as the teaching you have so done in his name?" Luther answered audibly "yes." And then he died in the early morning hours of February 18, 1546.

In the Roman Catholic understanding of death, the Devil seeks to tempt and mislead a person in their dying hour one last time. If someone succumbed to this temptation—for example, doubted God or had thoughts of revenge—they went to hell, regardless of how many good works or pious prayers they had amassed during their lifetime. For these highly dramatic eternity-deciding moments on the deathbed, the individual needed the last rites of confession and communion, blessed by a consecrated priest. That was also the popular, prevailing belief thirty years after 1517. But Luther had vehemently contested that! "Only by faith" does one enter heaven, "only Christ" saves from sin, "the grace of God alone" is enough!

So there wasn't confession nor communion at Luther's deathbed (and also, by the way, no parting words to his three sons who were present, no last greeting to Katharina, or anything similar). The people wanted to know then whether Luther really died "blessed." The ultimate reliability of the new evangelical faith was at stake! Justus Jonas had to hurry. Already one hour after Luther's death, he wrote a confession and sent it by courier to Wittenberg. To inform Katharina and the multitude of friends in Luther's house, certainly. In particular, however, he was in haste with his "press release" to try to prevent the bad PR that in the following decades could not to be prevented: targeted and widely disseminated rumors by his opponents.

According to Rome, Luther died as a heretic, and the incarnate Satan picked him up on February 18. Luther supposedly died of alcohol poisoning. Luther killed himself due to despair, then his servant supposedly found "our Sir Martin hanging on the bed and strangled miserably."[7]

While Luther was posthumously demonized, he was, of course, deified as well: in 1546, the first "fans" already made a pilgrimage to the house where he died and secretly hacked off a couple shavings from Luther's deathbed because they were supposed to help toothaches. In 1707, the clergy in Eisleben had what was left of Luther's bed after 150 years officially burned! To curb the very unevangelical cult of relics!

In Justus Jonas's death report, one reads that Luther died in the apartment of the town clerk, Johann Albrecht, in "Doctor Drachstädt's house." In 1726, the city chronicle writer Christian Francke confused this with the house of a Bartholomäus Drachstädt at Andreas Church Square 7. There stands over the door entrance even today: "In this house died Dr. Martin Luther on February 18, 1546."

Well, yes, but . . . in *that* house he certainly did not die.

The actual historical house where Luther died can be found at the address Markt 56. Which is where the district committee building of the Socialist Unity Party of [East] Germany used to be headquartered.[8] Perhaps Luther would have enjoyed the irony.

---

7. Ahrens, *Die Wittenbergisch Nachtigall*, 251.
8. Dieckmann, "Martini Himmelfahrt."

Chapter 23

Luther and His Wife Had Spectators During Sex

Once, yes. On the night of June 13, 1525.

So actually this is not a myth. In the bedroom with them were (at least) the jurist Justus Jonas and the minister Johannes Bugenhagen. But wait—before you puzzle over such a thing, shaking your head about whether it's right for other people to be in the room other than the loving pair, Martin and Katharina, let's revisit the sixteenth century.

As we understand the statement today, it's not a myth—there were witnesses. It was not, however, about sex in front of voyeurs, but about the nuptials or so-called "bed conduct." According to medieval law, a father's guardianship for his daughter passes to the son-in-law at the moment when they first get into bed, as is stated, for example, in a survey of Saxon law from 1220. The rights and duties of the young married man toward his wife and the legal claims of the young wife toward her husband took effect with their first sexual act. And it had to be certified by a notary. For this, one needed witnesses, "marriage witnesses" in the original sense of the word because whether the two were really married could not be assured in the church, according to medieval thinking, but rather had to be proven in bed.

"Luther took Katharina von Bora as his wife. Yesterday, I was present

146

and saw the couple lying on the wedding bed. I couldn't contain myself and shed tears at this spectacle,"[1] Justus Jonas said (a bit too sentimentally perhaps?) at a festive breakfast the following Wednesday morning. The touching "spectacle" normally followed a set ritual: the marriage witnesses escorted the specially attired couple into the bedroom. There was a short speech (as we know from the nuptials of Margaret of Brunswick-Lüneburg with her Johann Casimir, Duke of Saxe-Coburg: "Christian admonition, happening before the copulation on September 16, 1599"). Then the couple was undressed[2] and "tucked under their first shared blanket."

> "Therefore, I have now married as per the wish of
> my dear father and for the sake of these evil
> yappers am in a hurry to hold the nuptials."

Even for Luther himself, it was important to announce the consummation. On June 15, 1525, he wrote to the town councils of his hometown: "Now then, I want to make myself ready before my end [Luther was forty-two; life expectancy was around the mid-forties] and be found in the state created by God [to live as a husband], so that none of my early popish life [as a faithful-to-the-pope monk] is left over. Therefore, I have now married as per the wish of my dear father [at last! Hans Luther was against his son staying single] and for the sake of these evil yappers am in a hurry to hold the nuptials."[3]

For the sake of which "evil yappers?" (Luther is being playful here, no doubt.)

As a prominent figure, Luther was under public surveillance, more than ever by his critics and opponents. Of all people, the great humanist

---

1. Friedenthal, *Luther*, 536–37.
2. Wolf, *Luther*, 227. This was done in separate rooms with some modesty for both parties. The witnesses then withdrew to a respectable distance in the room or house.
3. Fausel, *D. Martin Luther*, 91.

Erasmus of Rotterdam spread the rumor that Luther was a bit of a womanizer.[4] In the small community of Wittenberg, one person alleged that Katharina had been familiar with the affluent son of a patrician, Jerome Baumgärtner.[5] Or with the clergyman Kaspar Glatz.[6] Just a few weeks after Martin and Katharina's official wedding, the gossip circulated that the pair *had* to marry because there was a little one on the way. In at least three letters, the relentless, rumor-mongering Erasmus wrote that "a few days after the singing of the wedding hymn the new bride gave birth to a child."[7] (Fortunately, Johannes Luther, their first child, was born exactly twelve months to the day *after* the wedding on June 7, 1526.) Even two hundred years later, a Catholic theologian claimed that Luther was "sneaking out of the monastery at night now and again to a widow's daughter."[8] Out of this came a little Andreas, whom Katharina von Bora accepted as her own, generous as she was. Nice, huh?

Actually, a child named Andreas did live for some time in the Luthers' house: Katharina's nephew, Andreas Kaufmann, the youngest son of her sister!

Luther gauged public opinion correctly: a man who had rebuffed the emperor and pope, refuted ancient dogmas, declared ancient rites as redundant, hung his monk's cowl on the nail, and then married—what could you expect from someone of this sort after all?

The rumor mill seethed. So he shut it down quickly by carrying out—officially—the correct nuptials with Katharina and . . . even talking about it himself.

Is there any cultural carryover of this peculiar custom today? Yes, at least two examples: in East European villages when the bedsheets are hung over the village street the morning after the wedding night, preferably with the bloodstain of the deflowering visible; and in the church, when the father of the bride "gives" his daughter to the groom. We may

---

4. Wolf, *Luther*, 226.
5. Ibid., 227.
6. Brecht, *Martin Luther: Ordnung und Abgrenzung der Reformation*, 194.
7. Erasmus, *The Correspondence of Erasmus*, 325.
8. Joestel, *Thesentür und Tintenfaß*, 25.

think that's just so much Hollywood kitsch nowadays, but it's rooted in the handing over of the father's guardianship of his daughter to the son-in-law. So it's really about something we seldom think of today: legal succession.

Instead of shaking our collective heads from the distance of five hundred years, it's worth considering the popular question of when sex is "pre-marital," or rather when a valid marriage begins. During Luther's time, there was no civil marriage. Nobody even owned a marriage certificate. The church wedding had only spiritual significance and not legal standing (this is still true in many countries today), and it "seems to have taken place first *after* the performed nuptials,"[9] the legal historian Jacob Grimm wrote in 1828 (and he was not telling any fairy tales). The actual "valid" marriage was the nuptial night, not the church ceremony. With Luther it was no different: he and Katharina had a brief courtship (one day) and consummated their commitment to one another that night. Martin and Katharina married "officially" in the church on June 27, 1525—two weeks after their nuptials.

---

9. Grimm, *Deutsch Rechtsalterthümer*, 441.

Chapter 24

Luther Recommended That Husbands Take a Second Wife

This myth—and it is one—has a fascinating as well as a typical origin (for Luther). Before his wedding on June 13, 1525, Luther was very much in-demand as a pastor for his students, his Wittenberg churchgoers, and a rapidly growing flock of advice-seekers from near and far. "I can hardly respond to every letter, so many matters and cases are up to my neck, especially regarding marriage and priesthood,"[1] he complained in 1524 to his friend Martin Bucer. That people were turning to monks (of all people) with their marriage, sex, and relationship problems—that hasn't changed in the last five hundred years in some church groups.

Luther even published texts giving advice: "A Sermon on the Marital State" in 1519, "Concerning Marital Life" in 1522, and "Concerning Matters of Marriage" in 1524. In addition to these were his table talks on the topic and thousands of letters. Of all the literature he produced, which consistently, fully, and undeniably makes the case *for* lifelong marital fidelity, there are only two quotes which one could use against Luther: a man once complained that despite all his charming efforts, his wife didn't sleep with him for years. Luther warned her with the words, "Now

---

1. Brecht, *Martin Luther: Ordnung und Abgrenzung der Reformation*, 95.

it is time for the man to say: 'If you don't want to, another will.' If the wife doesn't want to, the maid will come."[2] This was not a recommendation to the man, but a warning to the wife.

Trickier is another piece of advice, but in the opposite case of a sexually unsatisfied *wife*:

> Rumor has it I have taught that if a man can't fully satisfy the needs of his wife, she should run to another. However, I thus said: if a capable wife receives an impotent man in marriage and could take another and didn't want to publicly embarrass him, then she may say to him: "See, dear husband, you have betrayed my young body and moreover have endangered my honor and my soul's salvation. And because no marriage is between us in the eyes of God, I will allow myself to have a secret marriage with your brother or close friend, and you will keep your name so that your goods don't go to the children of an extramarital affair. Let yourself then be willingly betrayed by me, as you have without my will already betrayed me." I further taught that the husband owes it to his wife to consent to her marital obligation to have children.[3]

Luther obviously had biblical levirate or "brother-in-law marriage" in mind (Deut. 25:5–6), which is about the preservation of the family line. Were there such "modern" levirate marriages at that time? Probably.

Were the two men and the wife happy with the arrangement? Probably not. But if this Luther quote irritates us, we can still affirm this reality: Luther found impotence or the total refusal of sex to also be a form of cheating the female partner. Moreover, he thought a marriage that was maintained legally and lived platonically was always better than a public denouncement, wild cheating, and finally divorce. The economic future of the children (from the brother-in-law or friend) was thereby secured

---

2. Friedenthal, *Luther*, 465.
3. Zitelmann, *Ich, Martin Luther*, 15.

in that they were instituted as heirs of their (legal and social) father. The quote remains a zinger, no question. It is, however, fully clear that Luther gave it not as a norm, but rather in a dilemma, an emergency situation, and therefore it *didn't* infringe on the esteem of marriage and its worthiness of protection. Quite to the contrary.

Ethical tightropes, conflicts between pragmatic and conscientious decisions, balancing acts between healthy common sense and religious conviction, trade-offs and compromises—for the stern moralists these are all the appalling stuff of the Devil. An abomination. Rigorists and radicals hoped simple black-and-white answers were the right solutions. For Martin Luther, these were increasingly seldom since he was not only a father confessor for the "simple people" but also a pastoral adviser for powerful princes.

For example, Luther owed a lot to Philip I, landgrave of Hesse: in 1521 at the Diet of Worms, he sat on the side of the (Catholic) Emperor Charles V. Three years later, a U-turn: Philip promoted and protected the "Lutheran," prevailed against some eight thousand rebellious peasants in the Battle of Frankenhausen on May 15, 1525, expropriated the monasteries in Hesse, gave the money to care for the sick and needy, and in 1527 founded the University of Marburg, the first evangelical college in the world. In October 1529, Philip hosted the Marburg Colloquy between the (divided) reformers Martin Luther and Ulrich Zwingli because he wanted to unite the young and fragile movement.

Good for Luther. But in December 1539, Luther's fellow combatant, Martin Bucer, sat suddenly at the table and let it be known that the landgrave had a problem of conscience: for the past fifteen years, he had been married to Christine of Saxony and had seven children with her, but he was desperately unhappy. Now he had fallen in love. With a nineteen-year-old Saxon lady-in-waiting, Margarete von der Saale. To have her as a mistress (which was common for nobles and would not have been particularly defamatory) was precipitating a crisis of conscience for Philip. For years already, he had not taken communion. Since honorable figures of the Bible had concubines—Abraham, Jacob, Gideon, Saul, David,

Solomon—would it not be possible also for him, Philip of Hesse, to marry Margarete legally as his second wife without divorcing Christine?

Luther consulted his friend Melanchthon and—refused. No chance. The polygamy of the ancient, nomadic Hebrew tribes was not adequate as a theological rationale for a parallel marriage today. But Luther gave Philip "confessional advice" under the seal of secrecy: the will of God is, and remains, faithful cohabitation with one's wife. However, instead of falling into "wicked harlotry" and a "tormenting of conscience," Philip and Margarete could privately view their relationship as marriage, even when that was not to be justified theologically, juristically, nor publicly.

"When one has a lover whom he cannot publicly marry without risk, and both have secretly sworn faithfulness to one another, that is a just marriage in God's eyes. And although it will cause trouble, such annoyances don't do any harm."[4]

However, Landgrave Philip had severe political and diplomatic consequences to fear. And apart from that, Luther later wrote to him, "I know well indeed to distinguish by God's grace between what can be allowed by God in moral dilemmas and what apart from such dilemmas, in reality and according to the order of the world, is not right in God's eyes!"[5]

Luther didn't recommend taking a second wife, but rather halfheartedly allowed it for an ally. And despite receiving an invitation, he didn't show up to the wedding. Bucer and Melanchthon did: they were there as Landgrave Philip and Margarete von der Saale were wedded in Rothenburg on March 4, 1540.

---

4. Krumbholz, *Euch stoßen*, 112.

5. Mayer, *Martin Luther*, 263.

Chapter 25

Luther Was an Anti-Semite

Of all the issues surrounding Martin Luther, reformer and preacher, the question of anti-Semitism is perhaps the most critical and the one wrought with the most lasting impact. Unfortunately, it is not a myth. Yes, this is true: Luther was an anti-Semite.

But merely uttering the sentence "Luther was an anti-Semite" is not exactly correct because he didn't oppose Jews racially as a people or a cultural community. Instead, his hatred of the Jews was religiously and theologically motivated. "Luther was anti-Judaism" would be more correct. It is an important distinction, as we shall see later. This, however, doesn't make his beliefs any less appalling.

In 1543, three years before his death, he wrote a treatise entitled *On the Jews and Their Lies*. In it, he recommended that their synagogues be burned to the ground, that their houses be destroyed, that their prayer books be taken away, that they be forbidden to lend money and receive interest, and that they be forced to perform manual labor.[1] How did Luther come to the point of issuing such a piece of "hate mail," which even shortly after its publication was embarrassing for some of Luther's friends and elicited the fierce objection of the Frankish reformer Andreas

---

1. Luther, *On the Jews and Their Lies*, 166–68, 197.

Osiander (1498–1552)? Just twenty years before, Luther had spoken out *against* the oppression of the Jewish population, against forced conversion and forced baptism, and *for* their political toleration in his essay "That Jesus Christ Was Born a Jew." If the Jews had not changed, what changed in Martin Luther?

Theologically, Luther viewed the Jews as those who disregarded and killed God's messenger, the Messiah, the savior Jesus Christ. He pulled this theological motive for his hostility toward the Jews directly out of the parables of the New Testament:

> "Last of all, he sent his son to them. 'They will respect my son,' he said.
>
> "But when the tenants saw the son, they said to each other, 'This is the heir. Come, let's kill him and take his inheritance.' So they took him and threw him out of the vineyard and killed him.
>
> "Therefore, when the owner of the vineyard comes, what will he do to those tenants?"
>
> "He will bring those wretches to a wretched end," they replied, "and he will rent the vineyard to other tenants, who will give him his share of the crop at harvest time." (Matt. 21:37–41)

From 1522 onward, such Bible passages were read by tens of thousands of Luther's followers (and his detractors) for the first time in German. And they even made a simple rhyme out of it: God damned his "old" people, the Jews, and chose a "new" people, the Christians. Many thought in the sixteenth century it was the Jews' own fault since the hooting lynch mob had demanded the crucifixion of Jesus against the will of the Roman prefect Pontius Pilate and took on the responsibility for this injustice: "His blood is on us and on our children!" (Matt. 27:25).

Sadly, Luther took this to the extreme: "Well then, let's just make sure that the blood passes on to their children." So he is reported to have said in his table talks, reflecting the majority opinion and general sentiment of Luther's contemporary culture. Jews were refused membership to the craftsman guilds. Their children didn't receive any apprenticeships as carpenters, bakers, blacksmiths, furriers, coopers, tailors, or shoemakers, thus shutting them out of common trades. Many young Jews made up for this exclusion from practical careers by pursing higher courses of education and were successful at foreign universities. They excelled in learned languages, promoted and explored art and science, and conducted international commerce as agents and brokers, in which they loaned money and lived off interest. Their success, however, merely served to breed further hostility.

The result, overly simplified and generalized, was: in Luther's day Jews were in most cases more educated and richer than the average person. This led to an amplified hatred of the "elite" and encouraged—especially on Good Friday, the day of Jesus's crucifixion—pogroms: all-out riots of bloodlust featuring looting, plunder, arson, and murder.

When long-established and familiar securities broke away in Europe— and to this Luther had significantly contributed—and society itself became increasingly differentiated, then the calls to unity, solidarity, and identity began to ring loudly. And as history has shown time and time again, what unites frightened people more than a fight against a common enemy? Populists and demagogues of all centuries distinguish first and foremost between "us"—the threatened good guys—and "them"—the bad guys. Unfortunately, it works the same even today. And in the troubled early sixteenth century, there were two very accessible enemies. On the foreign policy front, Turks were encroaching from the Balkans. The internal—and nearer—threat was the Jews.

Martin Luther was, on the one hand, enough of an intellectual not to be fooled by crude racism. When the Catholic church forbade intermarriage between Jews and Christians, Luther scoffed: "Marriage is an external, worldly thing. Since I can now eat, drink, sleep, go, ride, buy, speak, and deal with a heathen, Jew, Turk, or heretic, then I can also be married to one and remain so. Don't bother yourself with the laws of fools, which forbid such a thing."[2]

On the other hand, Martin Luther was, in many ways, a complete

---

2. Luther, *Vom ehelichen Leben*, 24.

child of his time, trapped by the prevailing way of thinking, in which even intellectuals believed the most abstruse and obtuse conspiracy theories. The Catholic theology professor Johann Eck preached, for example, that Jews used the blood of Christian children for baking the matzo for the Passover feast.[3] In comparison, Martin Luther sounded moderate when he thought that Germany should follow the example of England, France, and Spain and deport the Jews legally.

> "Marriage is an external, worldly thing. Since I can now eat, drink, sleep, go, ride, buy, speak, and deal with a heathen, Jew, Turk, or heretic, then I can also be married to one and remain so."

However, after more than twenty years of advocating for fair treatment for the Jews (and their conversion to Christianity), Luther's attitudes hardened. The Jews, it seemed, had been abandoned by God and were beyond redemption. "Now just behold these miserable, blind, and senseless people. . . . Their blindness and arrogance are as solid as an iron mountain."[4] And it was to grow worse as Luther's own health went from bad to worse. In the three short years before his death, Luther himself became hard as iron. In his last sermon, three days before his death in 1546, he proclaimed,

> They are our public enemies. They do not stop blaspheming our Lord Christ, calling the Virgin Mary a whore; Christ, a bastard; and us changelings or abortions. If they could kill us all, they would gladly do it. . . . Yet, we will show them Christian love and pray for them that they may be converted to receive the Lord, whom they should properly honor more than we. Whoever will

---

3. Kaufmann, "Bitte verramscht Luther nicht!," 17.
4. Luther, *On the Jews and Their Lies*, 29, 38.

not do this is no doubt a malicious Jew, who will not stop blas-
pheming Christ, draining you dry, and, if he can, killing [you].[5]

Would that Luther's repugnant theology had died in the ensuing
years! Sadly, another monstrosity of history made sure that Luther's horrible treatise *On the Jews and Their Lies* became well known by quoting
it, distributing it, and celebrating it.[6] That monster, of course, was the
Nazi Party under Adolf Hitler. With a campaign of violence and intimidation, the Nazis won a plurality in the Reichstag, Germany's parliament, in November 1932. Hitler formed a coalition government and was
appointed chancellor in January 1933. Shortly thereafter, the Reichstag
building caught fire, an act blamed on Communists. Through legal political maneuverings as well as further intimidation and violence, Hitler
passed the Enabling Act of 1933 that made him the virtual dictator of
Germany. (The words "seizing power" still sound as if the poor German
people couldn't have done anything about it.)

The Nazis celebrated Luther's 450th birthday (he was born in 1483)
with a swastika poster and the slogan "Hitler's Struggle and Luther's
Sense are the German People's Defense." On November 9–10, 1938, the
first Nazi-led mass violence against the Jews began on Kristallnacht (also
known as the Night of Broken Glass) as a barbaric medieval pogrom
against defenseless Jewish citizens raged through the streets. Jews were
attacked and murdered, hundreds of synagogues were burned, and thousands of Jewish businesses looted. Among other inspirations for their acts,
the perpetrators called upon Martin Luther:

> One leading Protestant churchman, Bishop Martin Sasse, pub-
> lished a compendium of Martin Luther's anti-Semitic vitriol
> shortly after Kristallnacht's orgy of anti-Jewish violence. In the

5. Luther, "Warning Against the Jews."
6. The city of Nuremberg (not aware of the bitter irony ahead after World War II)
presented a first edition to the arch anti-Semite Julius Streicher and publically dis-
played it in a glass case.

foreword to the volume, he applauded the burning of the syna-gogues and the coincidence of the day: "On November 10, 1938, on Luther's birthday, the synagogues are burning in Germany." The German people, he urged, ought to heed these words "of the greatest anti-Semite of his time, the warner of his people against the Jews."[7]

Julius Streicher, editor of the weekly anti-Semitic tabloid *Der Stürmer*, claimed at the Nuremberg trials on April 29, 1946, "Dr. Martin Luther would very probably sit in my place in the defendants' dock today, if this book had been taken into consideration by the prosecution. In the book *On the Jews and Their Lies*, Dr. Martin Luther writes that the Jews are a serpent's brood and one should burn down their synagogues and destroy them."[8]

So, is it true Luther should also have been condemned at Nuremburg?

No. No figure from history is immune to later abuse by ideological usurpation. Every historical figure must be understood in the context of the conditions and circumstances in which they thought. That the Holocaust did *not* have Lutheran roots, but rather secular, race-based ideological and political roots and found its source in an ethnic belief in the "Aryan bloodline"—this viewpoint was set forth by a German pas-tor in 1946, who had no reason to whitewash the Nazi regime: Hans Asmussen, cofounder of the Confessing Church in resistance to the Nazis and cosigner of the Barmen Declaration of May 1934 and of the Stuttgart Declaration of Guilt of the Evangelical Church in Germany of October 19, 1945.[9]

Of further note: we must consider the fact that Adolf Hitler, Gestapo chief Heinrich Himmler, chief propagandist Josef Goebbels, Auschwitz commander Rudolf Höss, torture doctor Josef Mengele, and

---

7. Goldhagen, *Hitler's Willing Executioners*, 111.
8. "Nuremburg Trial Proceedings Vol. 12," Yale Law School. The judges, however, found this hardly persuasive, and Streicher was hanged in October 1946 along with nine other defendants.
9. Konukiewitz, *Hans Asmussen*, 221.

"approximately three-fourths of the concentration camp command-
ers" were all Catholic, as the Jewish Nazi hunter Simon Wiesenthal has
observed.[10] Does that mean we should look for the roots of the Holocaust
within Catholic theology? No.

And today?

In 1983 on Luther's five-hundredth birthday, the Evangelical Church
in Germany denounced Martin Luther's anti-Judaism in an official statement as a "contradiction to belief in the one God." The Reformation
Jubilee 2017 is not concealing or sugarcoating Luther's hate of Jews,
either. On the contrary: "Perhaps never before has so much regarding
the Protestant hostility toward Jews been spoken about, researched, and
written about at such a high level as today."[11] The church parliament of
the state church in central Germany—in an area where almost all the
important Luther spots are located—"confessed" in fall 2016 the "faults
and shortcomings in our church, where theologically motivated hostility
toward the Jews was carried further and passed on even until the most
recent days, as if it was a part of the gospel."[12]

And in front of the Marktkirche (Market Church) in Hanover, a central place in the inner city, pastor Hanna Kreisel-Liebermann blindfolded
the Luther monument on November 9, 2016—the day commemorating
the Night of Broken Glass in 1938—"as a symbol of the blindness of the
reformer with respect to Judaism."[13]

And with that, there is nothing left to be added. Unfortunately.

---

10. Siemon-Netto, *Luther*, 18.
11. Holz, "Luthers Abweg."
12. Evangelischer Pressedienst, "Synode distanziert sich von Antisemitismus Luthers."
13. Evangelischer Pressedienst—Landesdienst Niedersachsen-Bremen, "Luther mit ver-
    bundenen Augen."

Portrait of Martin Luther in later life by Lucas Cranach the Younger (1515–1546)
Museum of Art History, Vienna, Austria

Bibliography

Abagond, Julian. "Money in Leonardo's Time." *Abagond*, May 10, 2007. https://abagond.wordpress.com/2007/05/10/money-in-leonardos-time/.

Ahrens, Donald. *Die Wittenbergisch Nachtigall*. Bergisch Gladbach: Lübbe, 1982.

Aland, Kurt, ed. *Martin Luther: Tischreden*. Stuttgart: Reclam, 1960.

———. *Luther deutsch*, vol. 9 of *Tischreden*. Göttingen: Vandenhoeck & Ruprecht, 1983.

———, ed. *Die Werke Martin Luthers*, vol. 10. Göttingen: Vandenhoeck & Ruprecht, 1959.

Altaner, Berthold, ed. *Theologische Real-Enzyklopädie*, vol. 18. Berlin: Walter de Gruyter, 1978.

Augustine of Hippo. "Enchiridion." In *Augustinus Aurelius: Ausgewählte Schriften*. Edited by F. Pustet. Bibliothek der Kirchenväter 49. Munich: Kösel & Pustet, 1925.

Benn, Gottfried. *Ausgewählte Briefe*. Edited by Max Rychner. Wiesbaden: Limes Verlag, 1957.

Bensing, Manfred. *Thomas Müntzer und der Thüringer Aufstand*. Berlin: DVW, 1965.

Bernhard, Marianne, ed. *Martin Luther Hausbuch*. Bindlach: Gondrom Verlag, 1996.

Birnstein, Uwe. *Argula von Grumbach*. Schwarzenfeld: Neufeld Verlag, 2014.

———. *Who is Who der Reformation*. Freiburg: Kreuz Verlag, 2014.

Böckenförde, Ernst Wolfgang. *Geschichte der Rechts- und Staatsphilosophie*. Tübingen: UTB, 2002.

Bornkamm, Heinrich, ed. *Das Augsburger Bekenntnis*. Gütersloh: GTB Sieben-
    stern, 1980.

Bornkamm, Karin, and Gerhard Ebeling, eds. *Martin Luther: Ausgewählte Schrif-
    ten*. Frankfurt: Insel Verlag, 1983.

Brecht, Martin. *Martin Luther: Die Erhaltung der Kirche, 1532–1546*. Stuttgart:
    Calwer, 1994.

————. *Martin Luther: Ordnung und Abgrenzung der Reformation, 1521–1532*.
    Stuttgart: Calwer, 1986.

Brüllmann, Richard. *Lexikon der treffenden Martin-Luther-Zitate*. Thun: Ott
    Verlag, 1983.

"Content." The Codex Sinaiticus Project. Accessed March 7, 2017. http://www
    .codex-sinaiticus.net/en/codex/content.aspx.

Dieckmann, Christoph. "Martini Himmelfahrt." *Die Zeit*, January 31, 2013.
    http://www.zeit.de/2013/06/Luther-Museum-Eisleben.

Dithmar, Reinhard, ed. *Durch Gottes Gnade bin ich wohlauf: Martin Luthers
    Leben in seinen Briefen*. Leipzig: Evangelische Verlagsanstalt, 2008.

Diwald, Hellmut. *Luther: Eine Biographie*. Bergisch Gladbach: Lübbe, 1996.

Ellinger, Walter. *Thomas Müntzer: Leben und Werk*. Göttingen: Vandenhoeck &
    Ruprecht, 1975.

"Engagement und Indifferenz: Kirchenmitgliedschaft als soziale Praxis." Evan-
    gelische Kirche in Deutschland, March 2014. https://www.ekd.de/down
    load/ekd_v_kmu2014.pdf.

Erasmus, Desiderius. *The Correspondence of Erasmus: Letters 1535–1657*. Edited
    by Alexander Dalzell. Toronto: University of Toronto Press, 1994.

Evangelischer Pressedienst. "Synode distanziert sich von Antisemitismus Luthers."
    Die Welt, November 20, 2016. https://www.welt.de/kultur/article15961908
    /Synode-distanziert-sich-von-Luthers-Judenfeindschaft.html.

Evangelischer Pressedienst—Landesdienst Niedersachsen-Bremen. "Luther mit
    verbundenen Augen." Evangelisch-Lutherische Landeskirche Hannovers,
    November 9, 2016. https://www.landeskirche-hannovers.de/evlka-de
    /presse-und-medien/frontnews/2016/11/09.

Fassmann, Kurt, ed. *Die Großen der Weltgeschichte*. Zurich: Kindler, 1971–79.

Fausel, Heinrich. *D. Martin Luther: Sein Leben und Werk*, vol. 2. Stuttgart: Hänssler Neuhausen, 1996.

Francis I, "Be on Guard Against Pursuit of Power and Wealth." Vatican Radio, November 8, 2016. http://en.radiovaticana.va/news/2016/11/08/pope_be _on_guard_against_pursuit_of_power_and_wealth/1270801.

———. "Letter of His Holiness Pope Francis According to Which an Indulgence Is Granted to the Faithful on the Occasion of the Extraordinary Jubilee of Mercy." Libreria Editrice Vaticana, September 1, 2015. https://w2.vatican.va/content/francesco/en/letters/2015/documents /papa-francesco_20150901_lettera-indulgenza-giubileo-misericordia .html.

Franz, Günther, and Paul Kirn, eds. *Thomas Müntzer: Schriften und Briefe*. Gütersloh: Gütersloher Verlagshaus Gerd Mohn, 1968.

"Frequently Asked Questions: Doctrine." The Lutheran Church—Missouri Synod. Accessed March 7, 2017. http://www.lcms.org/faqs/doctrine.

Friedenthal, Richard. *Luther: Sein Leben und seine Zeit*. Munich: Piper, 1990.

Friedrich, Ina, and Stefan Schank, eds. *Die besten Anekdoten*. Geneva: Lechner, 1997.

Goertz, Hans-Jürgen. *Thomas Müntzer: Mystiker, Apokalyptiker, Visionär*. Munich: C. H. Beck, 1989.

Goldhagen, Daniel Jonah. *Hitler's Willing Executioners: Ordinary Germans and the Holocaust*. New York: Alfred A. Knopf, 1996.

Grimm, Jakob. *Deutsch Rechtsalterthümer*. Göttingen: Dieterichschen Buchhandlung, 1828.

Heine, Heinrich. *Sämtliche Werke*, vol. 3. Augsburg: Bechtermüntz, 1998.

Henkys, Jürgen, ed. *Luthers Tischreden*. Frankfurt: Edition Chrismon, 2003.

Holz, Klaus. "Luthers Abweg." *ZEIT Online*, December 8, 2016. http://www .zeit.de/2016/49/reformation-martin-luther-kirche-antisemitismus.

Hörster, Gerhard. *Markenzeichen bibeltreu: Die Bibel richtig verstehen, auslegen, anwenden*. Witten: Bundes Verlag, 1990.

Hürlimann, Martin, ed. *Martin Luther: Dargestellt von seinen Freunden und Zeitgenossen*. Berlin: Atlantis Verlag, 1933.

Joestel, Volkmar. *Legenden um Luther*. Berlin: Schelzky & Jeep, 1992.

———. *Thesentür und Tintenfaß: Legenden um Martin Luther*. Berlin: Schelzky & Jeep, 1999.

Kaufmann, Thomas. "Bitte verramscht Luther nicht!" *Idea Spektrum* 44, November 2, 2016: 16–19.

Kleinschmidt, Karl. *Martin Luther*. Berlin: Kongress-Verlag, 1953.

Konukiewitz, Enno. *Hans Asmussen: Ein lutherischer Theologe im Kirchenkampf.* Die Lutherische Kirche: Geschichte und Gestalten 6. Gütersloh: Mohn 1984.

Kopp, Eduard. "Horoskop und Genesis." *Chrismon*, September 24, 2010. http://chrismon.evangelisch.de/artikel/2010/horoskop-und-genesis-1906.

Köthe, Karl. *Martin Luther und Luthergedenkstätten in und um Eisenach*. Leipzig: Kranichborn, 1994.

Krumbholz, Eckart. *Euch stoßen, daß es krachen soll*. East Berlin: Der Morgen, 1983.

Kunst, Hermann. *Luther und der Krieg*. Stuttgart: Evangelisches Verlagswerk, 1968.

Landgraf, Wolfgang. *Martin Luther: Reformator und Rebell*. Berlin: Neues Leben, 1981.

Luther, Johannes. *Legenden um Luther*. Berlin: Walter de Gruyter, 1933.

Luther, Martin. *D. Martin Luther's Werke: Kritische Gesamtausgabe (Weimarer Ausgabe)*. 121 vols. Weimar: Hermann Böhlau, 1883–2009.

———. *First Principles of the Reformation, or The 95 Theses and the Three Primary Works of Dr. Martin Luther*. Translated by Henry Wace and C. A. Buchheim. London: John Murray, 1883.

———. *Martin Luthers Sämtliche Schriften*. Edited by Johann Georg Walch. Groß Oesignen: Lutherischen Buchhandlung, 1986.

———. *On the Jews and Their Lies*. Edited by Domenico d'Abruzzo. Charleston: CreateSpace, 2015.

———. "Preface." In *The Complete Edition of Luther's Latin Works (1545)*. Translated by Andrew Thornton. Originally published as *Luthers Werke in Auswahl*, vol. 4. Edited by Otto Clemen. 6th ed. Berlin: Walter de Gruyter, 1967. https://www.iclnet.org/pub/resources/text/wittenberg/luther/preflat-eng.txt.

————. *Tischreden*. Edited by Kurt Aland. Stuttgart: Reclam, 1960.

————. *Vom ehelichen Leben*. Wittenberg: Rhau-Grunenberg, 1522.

————. "Warning Against the Jews." Wikisource, January 21, 2016. https://
en.wikisource.org/wiki/Translation:Warning_Against_the_Jews.

————. *Wider Hans Worst*. Glaubensstimme: Das evangelische Archiv im Internet. Accessed March 31, 2017. http://www.glaubensstimme.de/doku
.php?id=autoren:l:luther:w:wider_hans_worst.

Maess, Thomas, ed. *Dem Luther aufs Maul geschaut*. Leipzig: Koehler & Ame-
lang, 1982.

Mayer, Hans. *Martin Luther: Leben und Glaube*. Gütersloh: Gütersloher Verlagshaus, 1982.

Mehring, Franz. *Gesammelte Schriften*, vol. 5a. Berlin: Dietz, 1975.

Mieder, Wolfgang. "Ist das jetzt spruchreif?" By Matthias Kalle. *ZEIT Online*,
November 17, 2011. http://www.zeit.de/2011/47/Sprichwoerter-Interview
-Mieder.

Möller, Bernd. *Deutschland im Zeitalter der Reformation*. Deutsche Geschichte
4. Göttingen: Vandenhoeck & Ruprecht, 1999.

Moore, David W. "One in Four Americans Superstitious." Gallup, October 13,
2000. http://www.gallup.com/poll/2440/one-four-americans-superstitious
.aspx.

Müller, J. T., ed. *Die symbolischen Bücher der evangelisch-lutherischen Kirche*.
Stuttgart: Liesching, 1860.

"Musste Margot Käßmann unbedingt zurücktreten?" *Die Welt*, February 25,
2010. https://www.welt.de/News/article6555244/Musste-Margot-Kaess
mann-unbedingt-zuruecktreten.html.

Neumann, Hans-Joachim. *Luthers Leiden: Die Krankengeschichte des Reformators*, Berlin: Wichern, 1995.

"Nuremburg Trial Proceedings Vol. 12: One Hundred and Sixteenth Day, Mon-
day, 29 April 1946." Yale Law School, Lillian Goldman Law Library,
2008. http://avalon.law.yale.edu/imt/04-29-46.asp.

Oberman, Heiko A. *Luther: Man Between God and the Devil*. Translated by
Eileen Walliser-Schwarzbart. New Haven: Yale University Press, 1989.

Peltzer, Karl. *Das treffende Zitat*. Bindbach: Gondrom, 1997.

Piltz, Georg. *Daher bin ich*. Leipzig: F. A. Brockhaus Verlag, 1983.

Prause, Gerhard. *Niemand hat Kolumbus ausgelacht: Fälschungen und Legenden der Geschichte*. Düsseldorf: Econ, 1995.

Reiners, Ludwig. *Stilkunst: Ein Lehrbuch deutscher Prosa*. Munich: C. H. Beck, 1991.

Renner, Rolf Günter, ed. *Klassiker deutschen Denkens*, vol. 2. Freiburg: Herder, 1992.

Saager, Adolf, ed. *Luther-Anekdoten*. Stuttgart: Verlag von Robert Lutz, 1917.

Schilling, Johannes. *Luther zum Vergnügen*. Stuttgart: Reclam, 2008.

Schloemann, Martin. *Luthers Apfelbäumchen?* Göttingen: Vandenhoeck & Ruprecht, 1994.

Schmidt-König, Fritz. *Käthe Luther: Die Weggenossin des Reformators*. Lahr: St. Johannis-Druckerei, 1983.

Schorlemmer, Friedrich. *Hier stehe ich: Martin Luther*. Berlin: Aufbau Verlag, 2003.

"Scripture and Language Statistics 2016." Wycliffe Global Alliance, October 2016. http://www.wycliffe.net/en/statistics.

Siemon-Netto, Uwe. *Luther: Lehrmeister des Widerstands*. Basel: Fontis, 2016.

Staatssekretariates für das Hoch- und Fachschulwesen. *Die deutsche Sprache: Lehr- und Übungsbuch für Ingenieurschulen, Fachschulen und Erwachsenenbildung*. Leipzig: Fachbuchverlag, 1959.

Stetzer, Ed. "A Closer Look: The Historical Reliability of the New Testament." *Christianity Today*, February 15, 2012. http://www.christianitytoday.com/edstetzer/2012/february/closer-look-historical-reliability-of-new-testament.html.

"Superstitions Held by Americans in 2014, by Religious Affiliation." Statista, 2014. https://www.statista.com/statistics/297176/united-states-common-superstitions-believe-religious-faith/.

Süßenguth, Mario. *Aus einem traurigen Arsch fährt nie ein fröhlicher Furz*. Berlin: Eulenspiegel, 2007.

"Temporal Punishment and Suffering." The Catholic Community Forum. Accessed March 7, 2017. http://www.catholic-forum.com/members/catholictracts/tract117.html.

"Toilet Where Luther Strained to Produce the Reformation." *Sydney Morning Herald*, October 23, 2004. http://www.smh.com.au/articles/2004/10/22 /1098316865171.html.

Van Flocken, Jan. "Wie Luthers Bibel unsere Sprache prägt." *Die Welt*, January 25, 2008. https://www.welt.de/kultur/history/article1590611/Wie -Martin-Luthers-Bibel-unsere-Sprache-praegt.html.

Vogler, Günter. *Thomas Müntzer*. Berlin: Dietz, 1989.

Wallace, Daniel B. "Earliest Manuscript of the New Testament Discovered?" *DTS Magazine*, February 9, 2012. http://www.dts.edu/read/wallace-new -testament-manscript-first-century/.

Winter, Ingelore. *Katharina von Bora*. Augsburg: Bechtermünz, 2000.

Wolf, Manfred. *Eine Frage noch, Herr Luther*. Leipzig: Evangelische Verlagsanstalt, 2004.

——. *Luther mal ganz anders*. Leipzig: Evangelische Verlagsanstalt, 2009.

——. *Thesen und andere Anschläge*. Leipzig: Evangelische Verlagsanstalt, 2005.

——. *Thüringer Porträts*. Gehren: Escher, 1999.

Zitelmann, Arnulf, ed. *Ich, Martin Luther*. Frankfurt: Eichborn, 1982.

——. *"Widerrufen kann ich nicht": Die Lebensgeschichte des Martin Luther*. Weinheim: Beltz, 1983.